Skyscrapers

An Architectural Type of Modern Urbanism

DATE DUE

MAR 0 1 2001		
APR 2 3 2001		
OCT 2 1 02		
OCT 2 8 03		
APR 2 0 05		
JUL 1 8 05		
NOV 0 3 0010		
APR 2 1 2008		

DEMCO 38-297

Mario Campi
Department of Architecture
ETH Zurich

Skyscrapers

An Architectural Type of Modern Urbanism

Birkhäuser – Publishers for Architecture
Basel • Boston • Berlin

This book has been kindly supported by:
Schindler Lifts Ltd, Switzerland

Schindler Lifts
Swiss Export Division

competence center

Schindler

Concept and realization:
Patrik Zurkirchen of the professorship Mario Campi
with Sandra Schweizer, Sarah Thury and Daniela Wirz

Design and production:
Werner Handschin, Birkhäuser Publishers
Christoph Kloetzli, Basel

Translation into English: Robin Benson, Berlin

Cover: Wood model of world
famous skyscrapers in scale 1:2000,
students work ETH Zurich, 1997/98

Cover photograph: Henry Pierre Schultz, Zürich

A CIP catalogue record for this book is available
from the Library of Congress, Washington D.C., USA.

Deutsche Bibliothek Cataloging-in-Publication Data

Skyscrapers : an architectural type of modern urbanism
/ Mario Campi. [Transl. into Engl.: Robin Benson].
- Basel ; Boston ; Berlin : Birkhäuser, 2000
ISBN 3-7643-6130-1

© 2000 Birkhäuser – Publishers for Architecture,
P.O. Box 133, CH-4010 Basel, Switzerland.
Printed on acid-free paper produced of chlorine-free
pulp. ∞ TCF
Printed in Germany

ISBN 3-7643-6130-1

9 8 7 6 5 4 3 2 1

CONTENTS

THE SKYSCRAPER – AN ARCHITECTURAL TYPE OF MODERN URBANISM

Constructing tall buildings, higher than their surroundings, towering above the city, structures that display and manifest themselves: for thousands of years now, human beings have been occupying themselves with this task. The Tower of Babel illustrates humanity's yearning to reach heaven, Pharos of Alexandria stands for control over the seas, the church spires symbolise religious belief and the medieval towers in San Gimignano are an expression of secular power. From time immemorial, people have invested their towers with iconographic meaning; and from the very start, they have attached both secular and religious, public and private connotations to their "skyscrapers".

Ever since I was appointed professor at the department of architecture at the ETHZ, in 1985, we have been examining fundamental questions of typology and morphology in the field of architecture. It was only logical, then, that the idea should have arisen during the academic year of 1997/98, enquiring about the nature of existing skyscrapers and, at the same time, having students design projects for the city of Seoul under the supervision of their professor. Our goal was to gain a deeper understanding of the conceptual properties of this architectural type, to determine its basis and establish how it came into use, as well as to assess how far we might be justified in talking here of a new type of building.

As an introduction to the subject matter, and to provide the students with comparative information on the fundamentals of skyscraper design, each student was asked to study an existing skyscraper during the analytical phase of the project. The building was to be considered under the following headings: urban context, structure, circulation/installations, and façade. The choice was determined by the urban context in which a particular building was situated, its distinguishing features, the decisive architectural development it represented, and the relevance, as well as the reputation of the architect who designed it. This skyscraper study intended to equip the students with a well-founded body of knowledge for designing their own projects and, at the same time, to let them do a comparative analysis of urban-planning principles, study structural systems and technical services, follow the form debate in architecture with the aid of manifold examples and, lastly, to consider all these aspects in relation to one another.

As architects and teachers we are primarily interested in the typological connections. According to The New Shorter Oxford Dictionary, typology is the "branch of knowledge that deals with classes with common characteristics". In the present context this means: structures, structural systems, use, circulation and form. Whereas in German-speaking countries typological analyses generally try to distinguish and classify different types of building, in Italian cultural circles the focus of analysis tends to be the history of architecture and the lessons it teaches us, since these are considered essential to understanding typology. The type of building is judged less by its specific characteristics than by those characteristics that constitute the structure as a totality.

When this research project began, the skyscraper was still seen as an independent typological structure. During the course of our studies, however, we gradually realised that this type of building was more complex than first impressions might suggest. Pure as well as hybrid structures exist alongside one another, whilst the characteristics of other types of building are taken up and assimilated. We frequently find ourselves dealing with buildings designed for multiple use; load-bearing structures deviate from the customary steel-skeleton frames and have even been developed into complex tube-in-tube systems. The façade design ranges from the masterful mise-en-scène of classical style to futuristically inspired forms and two-leaf glass and metal façades. Ground plans have been the subject of the most striking innovations. Strategically located and optimised core zones are designed to the greatest advantage and with the utmost precision in the interior of a building so as not to squander any well-lit space; containing the maximum number of lifts, minimised emergency stairwells, and service shafts, they constitute an irreducible repertory surrounded by a more-or-less free-span floor area. In fact, however, all these features can be found in other buildings, too, the difference being that skyscrapers have umpteen times as many storeys stacked on top of one another. Nor do their skins alone justify talk of types, since they also borrow from prevailing currents within architecture. Nevertheless, when it comes to the question of morphology, of external appearance, a new type certainly has begun to emerge, a type whose most conspicuous feature is the geometrical relationship of the width to the height.

It is worth noting that the skyscraper is clearly identifiable not only by virtue of its historical development and the specific approach to architecture it embodies, but also because it has an identity easily readable as an architectural type. By this I mean that the skyscraper is a manifest product of a historical development, a creation of the altered nature of our cities, and that it has often left its mark as an adequate urban response to the evolution of specific urban situations and the modern city in general; it has thus achieved legitimacy as a contemporary expression of modernity.

In centuries past, tall buildings always appeared as isolated phenomena. Building these structures was an arduous affair, and so was reaching the top of them. The invention of the hydraulic lift in 1853 gradually changed the hierarchy of floors. Until then, the first floor, the so-called piano nobile, contained the reception rooms and was reserved for the head of the household. The attic accommodated the servants. But this new technical wonder made it possible henceforth for very important or successful individuals to get to the top with ease and run the world from their penthouses. For quite some time, the most common modes of construction, relying on masonry and wood, allowed for structures of limited height only, and so the dream of realising the high tower had to wait.

A second invention, which occurred at almost the same time, radically revolutionised construction techniques: the iron skeleton. English engineer Joseph Paxton developed a metal-frame structure of iron and steel for his Crystal Palace in London. The frame was clad with glass, supplementing what had hitherto been a static conception of supports and loads by a more complex system of braces, flanges and torsion rods.

On the basis of these new technical achievements, the high-rise building began its inexorable advance in our cities. At the end of the 19th century, in what were still the very early days of the skyscraper, the Chicago School, influenced by such outstanding architects as Louis Sullivan, William le Baron Jenney and Burnham & Root, provided a crucial boost to its development in the shape of Leiter Building I, the Reliance Building and the Carson, Pirie, Scott Building. The inexorable advance of the skyscraper as a distinct type of building was soon accelerated by other factors too: the rapid cultivation of the American Midwest created a sudden rise in demand for working space; companies and department stores became increasingly dynamic and pushed their way into the market. Due to the concentration of buildings in the inner cities, the slowness of transport and the desire for

shorter connections, the cities were soon crying out for space; due to the enormous increase in land prices, owners, architects and engineers felt compelled to adopt the new technologies. These socio-economic changes, combined with the positive properties of steel-skeleton structures, which resulted in space-saving structural areas and rapidly assembled tubular scaffolding, transformed American metropolises like Chicago and New York into skyscraper cities. In this context, nor should it be forgotten that the symbolism inherent in skyscrapers, together with a frequently superfluous theatrical quality, a kind of antelitteram corporate identity, went hand in hand with a desire for social prestige, inducing investors to take the plunge and become builders as well as "owners" of these phenomenal buildings.

In terms of urban development, it was probably the Equitable Building dating from 1915 in New York that most decisively influenced the external form of future towers. Making the maximum use of available construction area and aiming to attain the most pragmatic height, it incarnated, on completion, the speculative interests of ambitious investors. The city responded with the New York Zoning Rules, which stipulated that buildings of this height had to be designed with set-backs and also placed strict constraints on the ratio between floor space and plot area. The first large-scale development in New York to cover several blocks, the Rockefeller Center, and even that surprising variation in urban development, the Seagram Building, where a plaza was created by setting back the building from the street building line, were an indirect and belated response to the Equitable Building.

Proceeding from the simple steel skeleton, the structural systems became increasingly sophisticated and were replaced by complex spatial frames. With their structural designs, ingenious engineers such as Pier Luigi Nervi, Ove Arup and Fazlur Khan, have ventured onto new territory, developing additional and more efficient systems.

The skyscraper has frequently served as a symbol of innovative solutions, as in utopian visions dealing with the problem of overpopulation, in attempts to capture spatial experiences in gigantic atriums, in conspicuous rooftops, or even in the endeavour to define distinct use zones. Such considerations, alongside technical progress and its consistent application, culminated in the veritable architectural icons of the Lake Shore Drive apartments by Ludwig Mies van der Rohe and the Price Tower by Frank Lloyd Wright. Mies' residential towers next to Lake Michigan, where structural logic is realised in the morphology of his building and announces a new era, were a pathbreaking development. However, wherever structural and design principles have been adopted and imitated by other architects, this has frequently led to the development of dehistoricised, faceless, box-like high-rise metropolises.

Again and again, the style of skyscrapers has been adapted to the architectural currents prevailing at the time of their design: the Chrysler Building to art deco, the Philadelphia Saving Fund Society Building to the International Style; even organic forms have manifested themselves in the outward appearance of other buildings such as Marina City. The consistent treatment of the curtain-wall glass façade at Lever House opened up new perspectives in the development of modern steel skeleton construction; the framed wall gave way to the curtain wall. The use of mirror-glass to cover entire façades made it possible to create naturally illuminated working and residential areas and, as in the case of the John Hancock Tower in Boston, to find convincing solutions for developing quite complex urban situations. In a similar way, purely functional approaches were tried out at the Nakagin Capsule Towers; high-tech aesthetics were adopted for Lloyd's Building; and in their buildings, the Postmodernists made bold allusions to skyscrapers such as the AT&T Building or the NationsBank. Nor should one forget the tricky geometrical feats performed for the Allied Building, or the seemingly infinite Tour Sans Fin, not to mention the colossal NEC Supertower and the Petronas Towers, both of which represent a corporate identity if not the identity of a nation.

What typifies the skyscraper more than anything else, however, is its capacity to be something very special whilst simultaneously purveying an everyday feeling in the urban context. The skyscraper contrives to present the public life of a private building in an urban context by adapting to the fabric of the city at the level of the street, whilst asserting itself in its own distinct manner on the vertical plane.

Due to its spaciousness, its splendour and the precise manner in which it is realised in the urban environment as the embodiment of a secular power or as the incarnation of an omnipotent state, the skyscraper never leaves us untouched. On the contrary, it compels us to take sides, to be for or against it. It is not easy to resist the fascination exerted by these giants among buildings.

Moving with the times without having to adapt to them, appearing ultramodern and always the subject of conversation – achieving all this is a true architectural art and lies in the essence of the skyscraper.

This most significant structure has succeeded magnificently in establishing itself as the very hallmark of modernity.

In closing, I should like to express my gratitude to all those who have been involved in this book. I should especially like to thank Patrik Zurkirchen for the invaluable work in assembling this publication, the students for searching for sources as well as for studying and evaluating texts and illustrations. I must also thank my assistants for editing all this material. My final thanks go to Birkhäuser Publishers for the confidence it has accorded me, particulary to Robert Steiger and Diana Eggenschwiler, and to the Schindler Lifts Company for generously sponsoring the project.

Mario Campi   February 2000

FLATIRON BUILDING

Location	New York, NY, USA
Architect	Daniel H. Burnham
Completion	1902
Height	87 m (285 ft)
Volume	ca 40 000 m³
Use	Office

Urban context

The unique form of this office building, which immediately induced people to baptise it the Flatiron Building, is created by the triangular junction at 5th Avenue and Broadway. This remarkable building is now Manhattan's oldest intact skyscraper and one of the city's landmarks.

The Flatiron Building, originally named the Fuller Building after its developer, was designed in Beaux-Arts style, a historicist building style (deriving its name from the Parisian Ecole des Beaux-Arts) dating from the 19th century. The twenty-storey building is reminiscent of a Greek column, subdivided into a base, shaft and entablature. The classical column is extended to form a wall that creates no impression of mass and depth owing to its sophisticated ground plan and rounded corners. The return to Classicism corresponded to a fashion prevalent in the United States – then emerging as a major nation – to shake off any sense of cultural inferiority vis-à-vis Europe. The building's eclectic ornamentation, which included elements of Gothic and Renaissance style, was promoted by the new millionaires in their endeavour to create an architectural incarnation of their social status.

Structure

The Flatiron Building was one of the first buildings constructed around a steel skeleton.

It was here that the shout "Twenty-three skiddoo!" became famous as the phrase with which the police drove away men who would gather and gape as women's ankle-length skirts were lifted by the strong up-currents at its base.

Circulation / Installations

Although the vertical circulation satisfied the demands of the time, it is rather modest by today's standards.

Façade

The limestone façade, which is rich in imitation Renaissance ornamentation, has slightly curving bay-windows in the centre. The barely two-metre apex of the triangle reminded the famous photographer Alfred Stieglitz of the bow of a huge ocean-going steamer.

WOOLWORTH BUILDING

Location	New York, NY, USA
Architect	Cass Gilbert
Structural Engineer	Gunvald Aus
Completion	1913
Height	241 m (792 ft)
Volume	ca 480 000 m³
Use	Office

Urban context

The architect Cass Gilbert was faced with the challenge of combining traditional aesthetics with the structure of a modern office tower. With the Woolworth Building, Gilbert succeeded in establishing an aesthetic principle that was to be binding for New York skyscrapers during the first quarter of the 20th century. The 59-storey Woolworth Building is located in the southern part of Manhattan, the Wall Street banking district. With a U-shaped base, 29 stories high, the building rises in a series of arches, turrets, struts and gargoyles, calling to mind Gothic style. Ultimately, it can be said that the Woolworth Building is a 20th-century building clad in Gothic details from the 15th century. It is an outstanding example of the American Beaux-Arts eclectic period. It is said that its owner, Frank W. Woolworth, built what for many years was New York's most imposing skyscraper in order to create an antithesis to the image of his "five-and-ten-cent" stores. Just like his cash-paying customers, Woolworth paid the entire cost of the building, which amounted to $13.5 million, in cash.

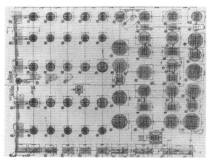

Structure

The load-bearing structure corresponds to that prevalent at the time, namely a steel framework with pillars and beams which have horizontal and vertical reinforcing. The structure is clad with polychromed terracotta.

Circulation / Installations

Coming from Broadway, one enters a cross-shaped, two-storey lobby-arcade with a barrel vault. With its lavish and somewhat eclectic ornamentation, combined with the very latest technical installations, this part of the building is a prime example of a then current conception of architecture aiming at creating prestigious works. Some twenty groups of lifts were arranged around the elevator corridor. Together with the installation shafts and the stairwells, these lift groups form the core area of the building.

Façade

With his masterly design of the façade, Gilbert brilliantly overcame the contradiction of a building entirely consisting of stories of equal height, all being used for the same purpose and having the same natural lighting, and, at the same time, having the stylistic elements, proportion and scale of Gothic architecture. Perhaps it was the cross-shaped lobby, the Neo-Romanesque ceiling mosaics, the Neo-Gothic elevator doors and letter boxes, or their combination, which induced the Episcopal bishop of New York to describe the Woolworth Building as the "Cathedral of Commerce".

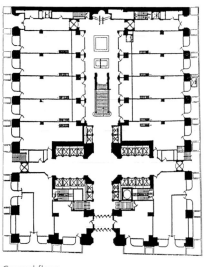

Ground floor

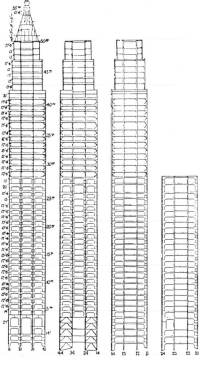

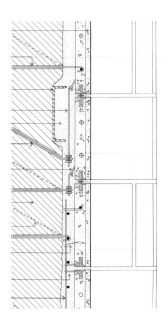

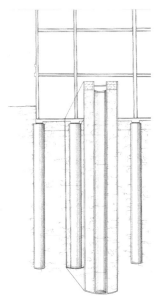

13

EQUITABLE BUILDING

Location	New York, NY, USA
Architect	Ernest R. Graham
Completion	1915
Height	166 m (544 ft)
Volume	ca 500 000 m³
Use	Office, restaurant

Urban context

In terms of its volume, which was determined by commercial considerations alone, the Equitable Building shows no consideration for its surroundings. The tower occupies the entire plot and owes its height to a formula aimed at creating an optimal relationship between the circulation area for the lifts and stairs, on the one hand, and the usable area, on the other. This plan triggered fierce controversy over the New York building laws after the skyscraper was opened. Consequently, the Zoning Law of 1916 was passed, which only permitted buildings of this height provided they were constructed on the set-back principle and thus reduced street shadow. Furthermore, a building's usable area was not to exceed twelve times the plot area. In the case of the Equitable Building, however, the usable area is thirty times that of the plot. The building's contribution to urban structures consists in its use of arcades on the ground floor, which bring urban life into the building.

Structure

The load-bearing structure consists of a flexurally rigid steel-framework structure filled with brick masonry.

Circulation / Installations

Competition from other buildings induced Ernest Graham to give the Equitable Building the most comfortable lift system in the world. The building's services and technical equipment play ed a very significant role in his considerations, since the possibilities offered by the lift system determined the height to which the building could be constructed. Originally, forty storeys were planned, subsequently reduced to thirty-six storeys served by forty-eight lifts. The lifts and the technical shafts are located in the middle section of the H-shaped structure. Great value was attached to installing the latest fire-protection equipment.

Façade

The façade conceals the structure of the building. It is structured in accordance with the classical system of plinth, standard storeys and crown-like apex. The design is clearly influenced by the Beaux-Arts tradition. Granite was used for the first three floors so that the tower harmonised with neighbouring buildings. The upper floors were clad in terracotta.

Interior view

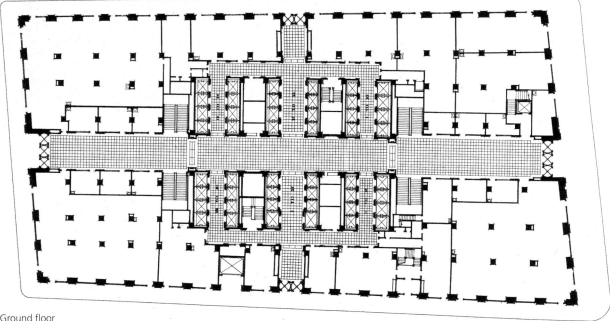

Ground floor

BARCLAY-VESEY BUILDING

Location	New York, NY, USA
Architect	Ralph Walker of McKenzie, Voorhees & Gmelin Architects
Completion	1926
Height	152 m (498 ft)
Volume	ca 250 000 m³
Use	Office

Urban context

The Barclay-Vesey skyscraper stands in the shadow of the World Trade Center. Designed by Ralph Walker for the New York Telephone Company, it represents a prototypical example of American Art Deco. This much-praised design helped the young architect to quickly become a partner in the renowned architectural office of McKenzie, Voorhees and Gmelin.

In terms of urban development, this was the first building to test the limits of the 1916 New York building regulations, introduced after the Equitable Building had been erected. The regulations aimed at greater safety and preventing ever-higher vertical skyscrapers filling the city, casting street level into a constant twilight. Application of the regulations resulted in the "wedding cake" stepped form, with limitations on height and with the body of the building rising in ziggurat style.

The building was supposed to be, as Walker put it, "as modern as the work of the telephone company inside". His design was governed by two basic ideas: firstly, that a good design is characterised by economy, and secondly, that a truly modern style is only possible using industrial production.

Part of the façade

The importance of this exceptional example of innovative architecture became apparent when it was chosen for the book cover of the American translation of Le Corbusier's architectural manifesto "vers une architecture".

The Barclay-Vesey skyscraper, with its daring, massive shape, emphasised vertical plane and flat ornamentation unrelated to any particular historical period and has come to be known as a masterpiece of early Art Deco.

Structure

The foundation of the building rests directly on the rocks of Manhattan Island, five stories below ground level. The excavation was secured with the standard caisson foundation. At the time of construction, the steel skeleton structure corresponded to the very latest state of technical development. While it was being completed, the walls and ceilings were installed. The building is reinforced by the central lift cores.

Circulation / Installations

Inside, a ground-floor passage traverses the building and connects West St. and Washington St. In the centre of the trapezoid ground plan, there are twenty-four lifts. Since the telephone company did not require natural daylight for much of its work, an atrium was not needed. The skyscraper houses shops along the Vesey St. side of the building, while the less important Barclay St. side has delivery bays with ramps.

Façade

The emphasis on the vertical piers, accentuated by the contrasting stone material, softens the striking set-backs. Like Sullivan, Walker favoured the use of ornamentation to make his architecture appealing and give it life. However, he did not employ meaningless traditional ornamentation but designed new organic forms, thus paving the way for the Art Deco movement. Rather than the height of the building being prescribed by some particular legal requirement, it was in fact determined on a commercial basis using cost-benefit accounting.

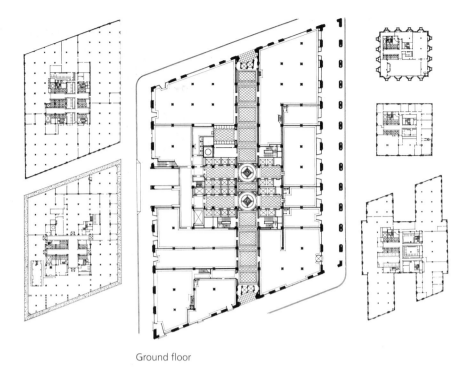

Ground floor

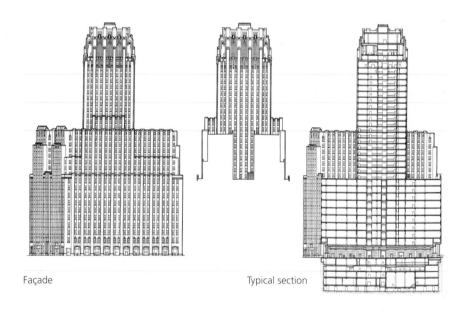

Façade   Typical section

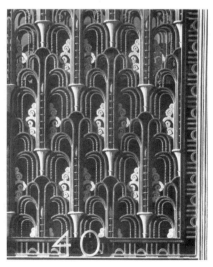

17

CHRYSLER BUILDING

Location	New York, NY, USA
Architect	William van Alen
Structural Engineer	Ralph Squire & Sons
Completion	1930
Height	319 m (1046 ft)
Volume	ca 350 000 m³
Use	Office

Urban context

For a long time, the Chrysler Building, which stands at the corner of 42nd Street and Lexington Avenue, was the tallest building in the vicinity. It is integrated into the city's strict street grid plan. The 3-storey ground floor, which has three entrances, occupies the entire plot. Application of the set-back principle made it possible to simplify the H-shaped ground plan of the plinth and create a rectangular plan. The building is crowned by a Nirosta-steel-clad spire from which a needle rises, formed from six arch-shaped steel elements. Classical composition (plinth, shaft and crowning capital) is given archetypal expression in the 70-storey Chrysler Building. The architect, who wanted to construct what was then the world's tallest building, resorted to a trick to fulfil his ambition. He kept all rivals in the dark about the true height of the completed building and had the steel spire assembled secretly inside the building. It was not heaved onto the top until the building was almost finished. However, his triumph proved to be short-lived, because the Empire State Building began to dominate the Manhattan skyline the following year. Even so, the Chrysler Building is considered one of New York's landmarks, and to many visitors its lavish art deco design makes it one of the most beautiful skyscrapers in the world.

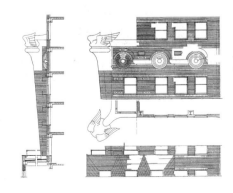

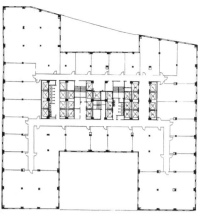

Typical storey

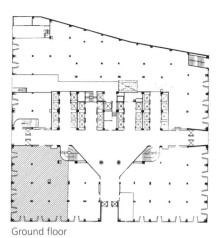

Ground floor

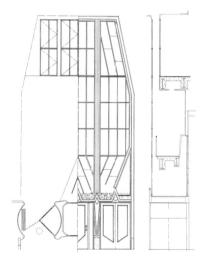

Façade detail

Structure

Adopting the static principle of a frame construction system, the load-bearing structure consists of a steel skeleton with columns placed at irregular intervals. Consequently, the façade does not have to perform a load-bearing function. The lift and the service core absorb the forces of the wind.

Circulation / Installations

The installations, which consist of four groups of lifts (with thirty groups each), two staircases and a fire-escape stairwell, are located in the core of the building. When the Chrysler Building was constructed, no other skyscraper was able to boast such modern technical installations. These included: a central suction ventilation system comprising gigantic rising pipes provided with suction valves to prevent dust entering; a novel power-cable system (laid in the floor) supplying all floors; incineration ovens designed to burn a half-ton of rubbish an hour; acoustically insulated steel interior walls that can be arranged as desired; individually adjustable thermostats on heating radiators (made of seamless-drawn copper piping) set back in the walls, etc.

Façade

The façade design strikingly emphasises the horizontal and vertical planes. Composed of black and white frost-resistant bricks, the façade displays a great wealth of lavish decorative detail. The plinth is clad in black marble. Relatively large apertures are placed at regular intervals on the lower storeys accentuating the horizontal plane, whilst the vertical is emphasised on the upper storeys. In the central, rectangular section of the building, comprising approximately thirty floors, the horizontals of the corners are accentuated by the long windows and brick courses, whilst the vertical plane is emphasised by perpendicular "fluting" in the middle of the façade. The building is crowned by six arch-like structures made of brightly shining Nirosta chromium-nickel stainless steel.

DOWNTOWN ATHLETIC CLUB

Location	New York, NY, USA
Architects	Starrett & Van Vleck, with Duncan Hunter
Completion	1931
Height	163 m (535 ft)
Volume	ca 96 000 m²
Use	Sport and recreation, hotel

Urban context

The Downtown Athletic Club exhibits a narrow rectangular form and has entrances on both Washington Street and West Street. Only the decorative design of the whole indicates the interior life of what is an unapproachable, highly abstract building. The exterior appears to be without any staged features, is not marked by changes of scale, and provides no indication of a potential bearing structure. The basic rectangular form is repeated unwaveringly on thirty-eight levels, although there is a slight deviation of form from the "original plot" of the ground-floor level as the building rises. With this appearance of continual growth – the only interruptions being formed by irregularly placed setbacks, creating the impression of tree-rings – the structure achieves unprecedented monumentality. This is not to be measured in terms of the contemporary comparison with the classical tripartite division into base, shaft and capital of a Beaux-Art aesthetic, which Starret and Van Vleck had already transcended 20 years earlier in the Barkeley Building. Inside the building one encounters a variety of scenarios, which unfold independently of one another within prescribed limits. Each level displays a scene from the "American way of life". "… Eating oysters with boxing gloves, naked, on the ninth floor – such is the "plot" of the ninth storey, or the 20th century in action" – a rendering in material form of proposition expounded in 1909. None of the levels is attributed to any particular purpose – a completely new

understanding of urbanity, and simultaneity in place of classification. The building serves merely as a framework for individual uses and no longer as a shell with a precise content. It is the guarantor of frictionless parallel functions. Architecture no longer has the task of developing scenarios, of manifesting values – planning can only limit life processes. Form is thus no longer the representation of a specific function, but is a direct translation of highly diverse, overlapping functions.

Structure

The frame of the building consists of a steel skeleton in which six column configurations can be distinguished. The positioning of the columns on the ground level indicates the principle direction of forces. All the setbacks in the outer walls are realised via complex load-distributing joist systems on a total of four structural floors. The floors of the first fifteen storeys also perform a load-distributing function.

Circulation / Installations

The lift structure on the northern outer wall forms the only continuum in the building. The lift does not assume any role in the scenery of the individual floors. From this observation point, the individual worlds open out for the visitor. An emergency exit stairway and an installations shaft are located on the side of the building.

Façade

The fenestration and the elaboration of the materials used for the façade, which is clad in red brick, call to mind the harbour buildings – the warehouses and market halls – that formerly stood near this site. Simply structured apertures with slightly recessed, massive parapets rise up the building, lending dynamics to an otherwise rather static-looking façade. The set-backs, required by the Zoning Rules, have been arranged to create tension-filled sequences of projecting and set-back sections, which have clearly been skillfully exploited in the room planning. As is the case with many other skyscrapers, however, no attempt has been made here to bring out the diversity of uses in the façade design.

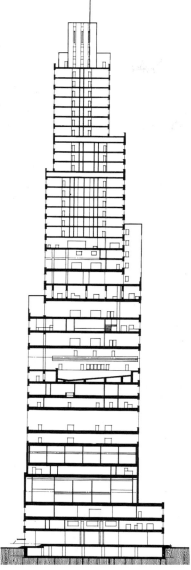

Typical section

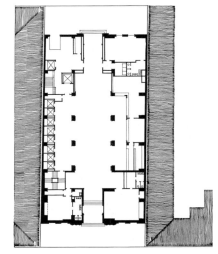

Ground floor

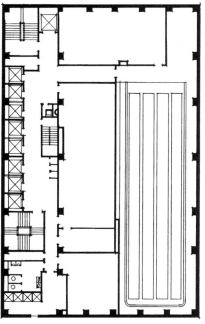

Swimmingpool storey

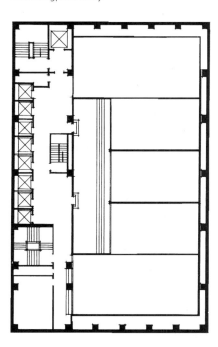

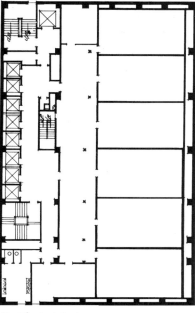

Squash court storey

EMPIRE STATE BUILDING

Location	New York, USA
Architects	Richmond Shreve, William Lamb and Arthur Harmon
Structural Engineer	H.G. Balcom
Completion	1931
Height	381 m (1,250 ft) (with TV mast 448 m)
Volume	ca 930 000 m³
Use	Office, observation deck

Urban context

The Empire State Building stands at the junction of 5th Avenue, 33rd and 34th Street on the site of the former Waldorf-Astoria Hotel. Although it was planned only as an object of speculative investment, the building was completed in the incredibly short time of eighteen months and proved to be a successful example of uniting a variety of functions.

The 5-storey plinth occupies the entire plot and forms the boundary to the street. Shops, as well as the striking 3-storey entrance hall to the elevator lobby, are located on the ground floor. Set back from the plinth the tower rises through set-back floors to the gently rounded tower at the top. For the entire height of the building, the sections were structured in accordance with the zoning rules. The Empire State Building not only became the symbol of the New York skyline, but of the skyscraper per se. A source of marvel to the population during the Thirties, it gradually became rooted in the New Yorkers' self-awareness. The film *King Kong*, with the love-crazed gorilla, certainly played its part, too, as did the pictures – later to become classics – taken by photographer Lewis Hine during the construction phase. Last but not least, right up until 1972, the Empire State Building was still the tallest building in the world.

Structure

The Empire State Building is a steel-skeleton structure with limestone infills and facing. Throughout the height of the structure, the columns are arranged on a continuous six-metre structural grid, with two 8-m trimmers at each of the side entrances. On the horizontal plane, the structural grid displays the following subdivisions: 10 m (A), 6.5 m (B) and 6 m (C), except for the entrance hall area and the two central lift groups, where the vault bays have a greater span. The large structural grid in the core zone of the lift lobby is continued up to the top floors. Owing to pressures of time and cost, it was necessary to use prefabricated steel components, which were riveted together on the building itself. The 67-m-high television mast was not added until 1950.

Circulation / Installations

The elevator lobby, with its sixty-four lifts, forms the core zone of the building. The shafts for the various media and sanitary facilities are connected to those for the lifts.

An optimal solution had to be found for the technical areas of the lifts and the remaining, rentable floor areas, which also meant developing the best lift circulation concept for the greatest ascendable height. Consequently, the lift design played an essential part in determining the form given to the building as a whole.

Façade

The shop level, which is clad in black granite, stands out clearly from the light grey of the limestone. Mullions clad in aluminium, a rare instance of art-deco ornamentation on this building, lend rhythm to the line of shop windows. On the upper floors, the darker colour of the windows, whose steel piers and aluminium parapets are set against the lightness of the limestone, draws contrasting strips on the building, lending emphasis to the verticals. Together, the materials form a unity of grey tones.

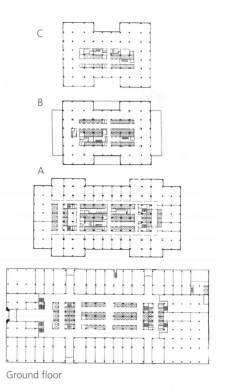

Ground floor

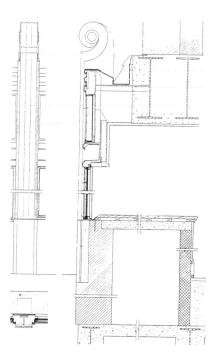

Façade detail

23

PHILADELPHIA SAVING FUND SOCIETY BUILDING, PSFS

Location	Philadelphia, PA, USA
Architect	George Howe & William Lescaze
Completion	1932
Height	150 m (492 ft)
Volume	ca 200 000 m³
Use	Shops, bank, office

Urban context

The Philadelphia Saving Fund Society building – famous for the initials PSFS on the roof – was a milestone in the history of American Modernism in the early 20th century. When the first exhibition on modern architecture was held at the Museum of Modern Art in 1932, the PSFS building, together with Lovell House in Los Angeles (designed by Richard Neutra and completed only a short time before) were presented as examples of what Henry-Russell Hitchcock and Philip Johnson referred to as "International Style". For Hitchcock and Johnson, this style had three decisive features: architecture is conceived in terms of volume and not mass; the composition is defined not by ornamentation but by asymmetrically arranged and rhythmically articulated uniform modules.

This complex, yet logically organised structure, is the result of an unconventional decision: to place the PSFS business offices on the second floor. This allowed shops to be located on the ground floor, thus not only providing rental income but also attracting new customers essential to the bank's business. A set-back and asymmetrically positioned T-shaped office tower was then built on the raised, unadorned bank floors. Only the 8-metre-high initials of the bank were displayed at the top of the tower, since it was assumed the full name would be indecipherable from street level. At night, the bright red neon letters can be seen from a distance of thirty-two kilometres.

Structure

The load-bearing structure consists of a steel skeleton. The steel columns, both inside and outside the building, are clad in stone. Above the banking floor, a room-high trussed girder transfers the vertical load from four to two axes.

On the upper storeys, the unit spacing is 6 m and 8.5 m; from the banking floor down, the unit spacing of the main columns is 19 m.

Circulation / Installations

The PSFS Building is constructed on a T-shaped plan. The offices are contained perpendicular bar of the "T", whilst the infrastructure for the entire building is located in the cross-bar. A novel feature of the design was that it openly displayed the infrastructure instead of stowing it away inside the building. With the air-conditioning system, sound insulation bricks and electric lighting installed in the ceilings, the PSFS Building was way ahead of its time.

Façade

The architects accentuated the verticals by displaying the piers, thus lending rhythm to the façade. Otherwise, the skyscraper has a modern, horizontal articulation. According to William Jordy, the uniqueness of the PSFS building lies "in its obvious, exceptional ambiguity, simultaneously representing reconciliation, synthesis, and prophesy." The approach taken by Howe, who was trained in the Beaux-Arts tradition, is combined here with William Lescaze's manifest allegiance to functionalism and technology.

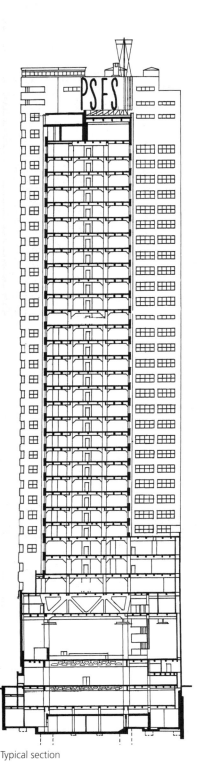

Typical section

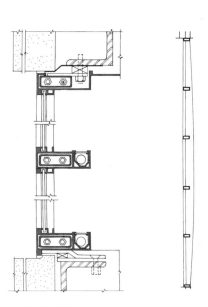

Window detail

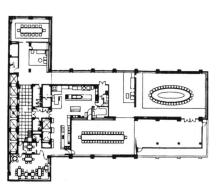

Meeting storey

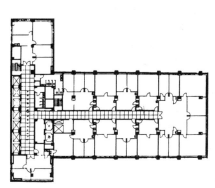

Typical storey

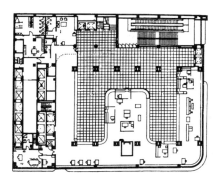

PSFS business office storey

ROCKEFELLER CENTER

Location	New York, NY, USA
Architects	Hood, Godley & Fouilhoux; Reinhard & Hofmeister; Corbett, Harrison & Mac Murray
Completion	1933–1940
Height	259 m (850 ft)
Volume	ca 3 200 000 m³
Use	Office, shops, theatre, museum, TV station, restaurants

Urban context

The Rockefeller Center extends over three blocks: from 5th to 6th Avenue and from 48th to 50th Street. By implementing an urban-structural conception and evolving a new organisational form for the skyscraper, an endeavour was made to meet the demand for higher quality, light, good air and a view. A group of twenty-one single buildings was planned around a central point – the 70-storey GE (formerly RCA) Building – in such a way that all of these requirements would be fulfilled. Proceeding from these considerations, a novel plan was elaborated which guarantied sufficient light and ventilation with a room depth of 8.10 m. The group of buildings is centred on a bustling T-shaped plaza with good traffic connections. The numerous shops around the square have upgraded the complex. In addition, the plaza for the three flanking office buildings not only serves as an excellent setting but also links all the buildings of the Rockefeller Center via subterranean passages, cafés and shops. The sunken garden is used as a restaurant in the summer and as an ice-skating rink in the winter. Over 200 shops and service enterprises nestle between works of art and garden architecture. What captures visitors' imagination most are the publicly accessible gardens, which are located on the lowest buildings and provide

natural scenery. The Hanging Gardens of Babylon served as the model for the entire complex. John D. Rockefeller, Jr., founder of Standard Oil, commissioned the Rockefeller Center, which has also been referred to as a "city within a city" and "the nation's most successful urban complex".

Structure

The Rockefeller Center is a steel skeleton structure with a curtain wall in the column grid. Its installations and circulation are integrated into the central core.

Circulation / Installations

The attraction of the Rockefeller Center lies in its express lifts and air-conditioning system, which were a novelty at the time.

Façade

All the façades of the Rockefeller Center display the same cost-saving, sand-coloured limestone curtain wall, lending the building a coherent and uniform appearance. In contrast, the ground floor, the lobby as well as the walls, ceilings and doors of the complex, are decorated with various allegorical sculptures, frescoes and reliefs executed in a wealth of variations. The designers chose to use the pier system when designing the façade of the "slab" GE Building. However, on a building of this scale the piers tend to appear as flat stripes. Another feature deserving mention is the Rainbow Room – situated at the top of the GE Building – which provides visitors with a breathtaking view of Manhattan by night.

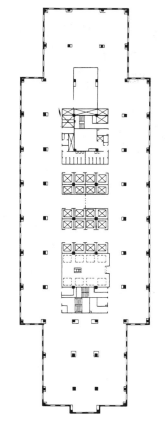

Typical storey

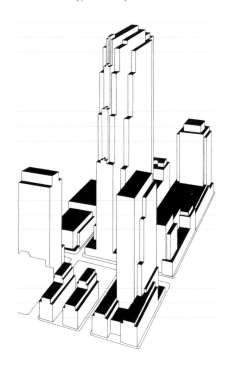

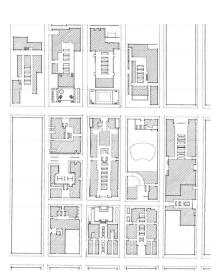

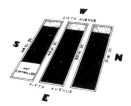

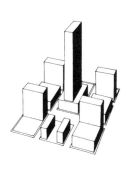

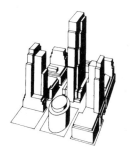

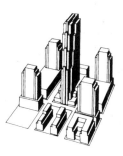

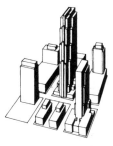

Urban context

JOHNSON WAX BUILDING

Location	Racine, WI, USA
Architect	Frank Lloyd Wright
Completion	1944
Height	46 m (151 ft)
Volume	15 000 m³
Use	Product research laboratory

Urban context

Following Wright's design, a series of roofed car areas were constructed to the north of the existing office building around a square courtyard. Their outer walls are of solid masonry and seal off the tree-like laboratory tower, rising in the centre of this "piazza," from the surrounding city. The upper section of the tower has alternating main floors – square with rounded corners – and circular galleries. All floors are developed from the core of the structure. Only the quadratic storeys are legible on the façade. The smaller circular mezzanines can be faintly detected behind the semi-transparent skin of glass tubing.

Structure

A reinforced concrete central core with a diameter of 4 m bears the load of the building is. The walls of the cylindrical core, which vary in width from 0.175 m to 0.25 m, support 15 storeys with a maximum cantilevering of 6.5 m. The façade does not have any load-bearing function. The foundation extends 16 m into the ground and, like the core casing, has a diameter of 4 m; it was poured without shuttering to ensure maximum anchorage in the ground. The storeys (75 m³ concrete), together with the matching core segment, were concreted successively in a single process.

Circulation / Installations

The core casing contains the elevator and the vertical supply piping. The building is fully air-conditioned. As the building is intended as a research laboratory, every floor is supplied not only with hot and cold water but also with distilled water, carbon dioxide, nitrogen and steam. The return pipes run through a separate shaft at the side of the stairwell.

Façade

Alternating bands of brick and Pyrex tubing, like those used in the first building, enclose the tower down to the ground floor. Behind the glass-tubing façade, additional panes of glass were fitted to provide protection against grime, water and wind. 113.5 kilometres of glass tubing were used for the façade.

The circular floors are visible through the semi-transparent skin. On the ground floor, the solid core casing is completely exposed, thereby accentuating its load-bearing function and sense that the slightly projecting floors are floating. This adds to the impression one gains from the outset that the Johnson Wax Company buildings were way ahead of their time.

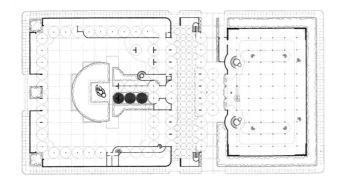

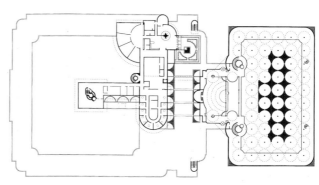

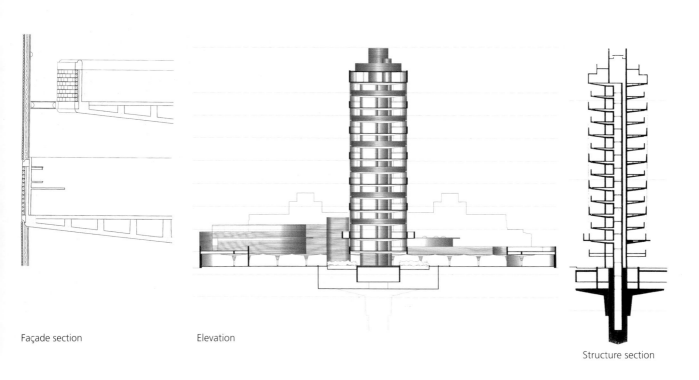

Façade section   Elevation   Structure section

860/880 LAKE SHORE DRIVE APARTMENTS

Location	Chicago, IL, USA
Architect	L. Mies van der Rohe
Completion	1951
Height	82 m (269 ft)
Volume	ca 53 000 m³
Use	Residential

Urban context

In correspondence with the city grid, the two identical 26-storey towers are positioned at right angles to one another on a trapezoid plot bordered by the diagonal shore of the lake and three streets. The residential buildings have a sculptural quality, are set back from the streets and appear as a solitary ensemble in which all eight sides are accorded equal status. The buildings were constructed in the same context as the 900 Esplanade apartments, likewise planned by Mies van der Rohe and erected in 1956. For various reasons, however, the 900 Esplanade Apartments were not executed with the same attention to detail.

In its absolute consistency of style, astonishing realisation and puritanical simplicity, this ensemble of two apartment blocks was a signal to architects in Chicago and throughout the world. It inspired countless architects designing high-rise buildings to imitate the example it had set – although not always successfully, it must be added.

Structure

The steel primary structure defines three fields on the narrow side and five on the longitudinal side, thus creating a quadratic grid. One of the fields, with a unit spacing of 6.4 m, consists of four aluminium windows on the non-bearing façade. The welded double-T profiles have load-bearing functions.

Circulation / Installations

Centrally located in the middle of the building are two access levels, one for each tower, with a staircase and a lift. Vertical shafts are located between the kitchen area and the wet room on the residential floors.

Façade

For safety reasons, the steel frame of the towers was clad in concrete. On the outside, the cladding was enclosed in permanent shuttering made of galvanised steel sheeting. Vertical standard sections of 20-cm-thick double-T girders (also used for the window units) were marked and fastened to the cladding. The concrete slab lining was reinforced so that it would bear loads, to reduce wind-induced movement and increase the so-called stay factor. The outer skin was inserted into 2-storey-high prefabricated elements (the quadratic principal axis having a width of 6.4 m) and welded to the load-bearing frame.

Subsequently, the light-coloured aluminium windows were mounted to the struts of the 1.6-m façade members. Uniformly light-coloured, reflective roller blinds heighten the contrast between the load-bearing frame and the glass infills.

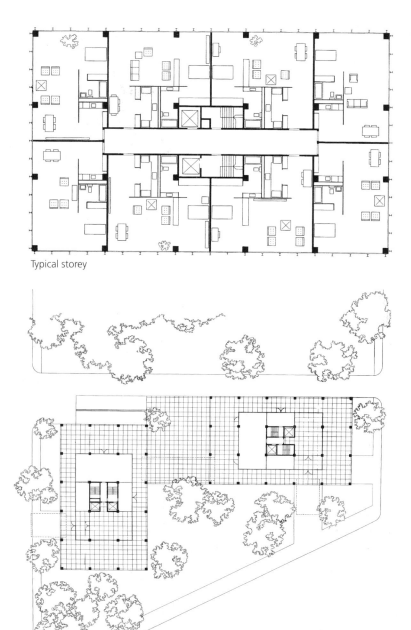

Typical storey

Site plan

LEVER HOUSE

Location	New York, NY, USA
Architect	Gordon Bunshaft of SOM Skidmore, Owings & Merrill
Structural Engineer	SOM
Completion	1952
Height	95 m (311 ft)
Volume	ca 105 000 m³
Use	Office

Urban context

Gordon Bunshaft made use of easily legible, tried-and-tested design tactics to create an aesthetically perfect volumetric composition, which, at the time represented an innovative example of modern construction with iconographic features. The main components are a two-storey horizontal plinth element corresponding to the plot area, and a tower rising from the narrow side facing the street. An interior courtyard in the plinth zone establishes a semi-private exterior space that skilfully creates an intimate atmosphere close to the hustle and bustle of the city. The idiosyncratic building constellation denies the edges defining the street space any ensemble-like qualities. Nor does it react to the customary scale of Park Avenue in the context of the street space and street edge. Consequently, when it was completed, Lever House stood out against the "old"-looking neighbouring buildings, considerably enhancing the urban quality of the location in combination with the Seagram Building diagonally opposite. The design makes use of traditional architectural solutions such as the clear sweep of the ground floor space, an over-dimensioned glass entrance hall and the atrium-like recess. Despite the lack of any concrete reference to its location, the vistas and the notion of returning space to the public domain

make the building adequate to its surroundings. It reveals its extraordinary charm in the cityscape in the day-and-night impact of the play of light it produces. As in the case of most other skyscrapers, the staging of interior themes such as rooms and circulation has not played a significant role in the design.

Structure

The building is a steel-frame structure. The plinth and tower support systems share a common basic grid. The support system facing Park Avenue is set back in both parts of the building, emphasising its self-contained volumetric character. The primary load-bearing frame is only visible behind the outer cladding and forms no edges to the building. The ceiling horizon is made up of a "Hourdis" cell system – common at the time – with a layer of concrete and light asphalt tiling.

Circulation / Installations

Vertical shafts contain two emergency staircases enclosed in separate cores, a group of 5 (increasable to 6) passenger lifts, a file lift system and the sanitation.

Façade

The outer skin consists entirely of heat-absorbent fixed glazing with interior roller blinds. It was not possible to install the floor-to-ceiling glazing originally planned due to the fire safety regulations, which required back-up masonry of parapet height.

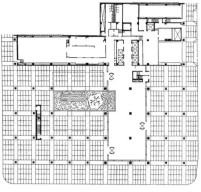
Ground floor

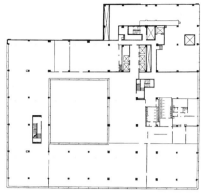
2nd floor

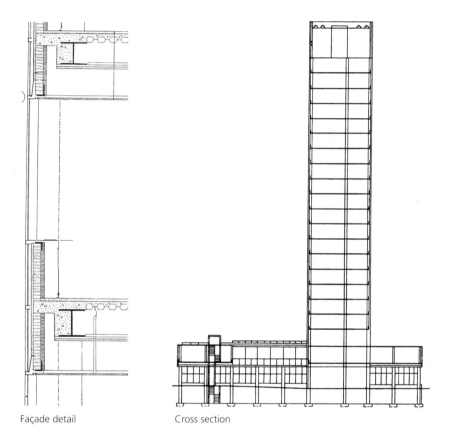

Façade detail

Cross section

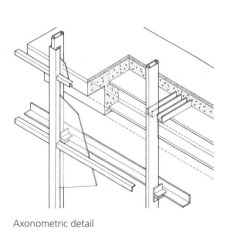
Axonometric detail

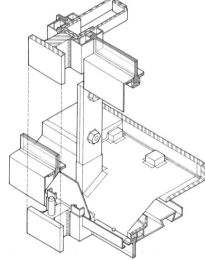
Axonometric detail

ONE-MILE-HIGH SKYSCRAPER

Location	Illinois, USA
Architect	Frank Lloyd Wright
Project	1956
Height	1600 m (1 mile)
Use	Services, office, residential

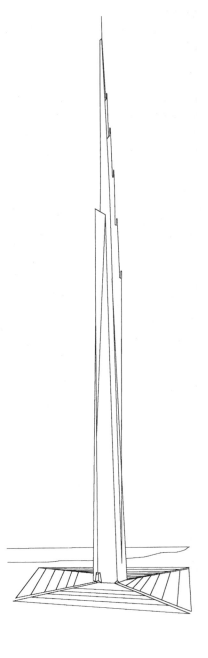

Urban context

Frank Lloyd Wright saw the design of the One-Mile-High Skyscraper as part of his plan, dating from the twenties, for Broadacre City. Existing cities were eliminated and replaced by suburban-type settlements with detached houses. Horizontal expansion was to be achieved by the generalised use of motorised transport and a developed road network. Skyscrapers were reserved for "incorrigible" towns and cities. With his One-Mile-High Skyscraper of 1956, he elaborated an urban focal point, a place that would meet societal, social and cultural needs. He changed his priorities in favour of creating an urban centre.

Structure

The load-bearing structure consists of a central tripod-shaped column, deeply anchored in rocky ground, and projecting plates – stabilised by steel ropes – resting on cantilevers. The building attains maximum extension at ground level in the keel-like basement and tapers like a hull at the plinth.

Frank Lloyd Wright believed that architecture ought to be organic. Hence, he compared his project with a tree consisting of a trunk, roots and branches. In his opinion, the central support would give the skyscraper a "natural" crown, because of the way the building tapered continuously to the very top.

Circulation / Installations

The technical equipment was to be located in the zone of the longitudinal support as a part of the core, but it was not developed in any detail. Nevertheless, the structure does display some striking features.

Thus, in a detail drawing, the tapering cantilevers are depicted as being hollow so that they could be used for the air-conditioning system, as well as for the power and water supply. Furthermore, Wright planned to install five-storey lifts running along rack rails, transporting up to one hundred passengers and driven by atomic-powered motors. In this, he was primarily interested in solving the problem of vertical transport and not in the spatial dimensions or the crowding that might ensue.

Façade

The façade shows an interplay of forces between the vertical lines of the lift shafts and the horizontal gradation of the parapets and windows. Wright elaborated a simple design for the façade so that the basic form of the building, with its interrupted triangular surfaces would have a visible impact. Gold-tinted metal was to be used for the cladding and the balcony parapets. For the windows, Wright planned to use Plexiglas, which was employed exclusively for aeroplane construction at the time.

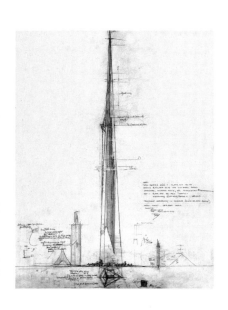

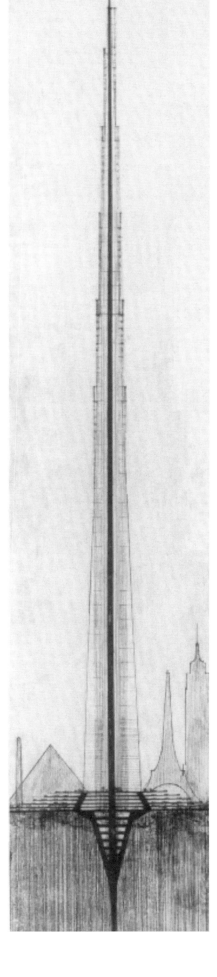

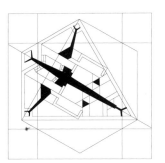

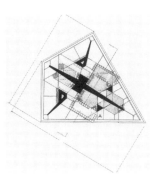

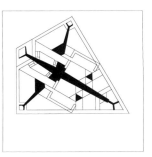

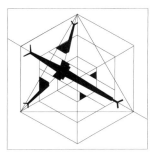

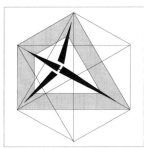

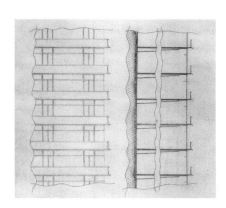

PRICE TOWER

Location	Bartlesville, OK, USA
Architect	Frank Lloyd Wright
Completion	1956
Height	56 m (184 ft)
Volume	13 000 m³
Use	Office, residential

Urban context

When designing towers, Frank Lloyd Wright proceeded from the same principles that had guided him in his designs for residential houses. He felt that skyscrapers only made sense if they were surrounded by an open green area and did not interfere in any way with life below. Wright believed that if skyscrapers were to optimally fulfil the demands of the Modern Movement for light, air and freedom, then they ought to be located in the countryside, where they would stimulate community life and prevent urban sprawl. The Price Tower, which is positioned on a hill in eastern Oklahoma, stands there like a tree that has fled from a crowded forest, i.e. the city. The tower, designed for the Price Pipeline Company, contains offices and maisonette apartments and represents a further development of the project for St. Mark's Tower. (St. Mark's Tower, constructed in 1929 for purely residential purposes, has four units per storey and a small park. Wright's building was erected with the same construction methods.) As the storeys are divided into four units, each apartment uses a fourth of the total floor area. The four top floors are reserved for the Price Pipeline Company only. Alongside the tower stands a two-storey building with company rooms. This building, which is open to the public, borders the site, shielding it from neighbouring developments.

Structure

The tower has a reinforced concrete structure with self-supporting floors projecting from the central core and diminishing in thickness towards the outside. The equipment and central access points are located in the core, which rests on a "pile-root" foundation. Mainly standardised, prefabricated building components were used. Only the concrete core and the concrete slabs were cast on the site. The partitioning walls inside the building rest on the slabs.

Circulation / Installations

The core contains four installation shafts located by the lifts. The rooms' lighting, air-conditioning and heating units are built into technical sub-floors.

Façade

The outside wall consists of a glass and metal skin, with sunbreakers, copper parapets and gold-tinted reflecting glass that are attached to the edges of the floor slabs.

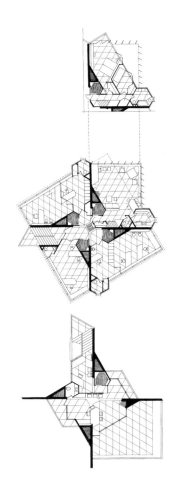

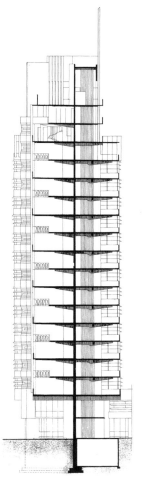

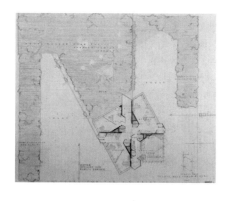

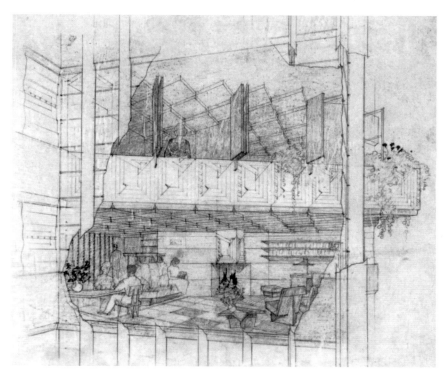

TORRE PIRELLI

Location	Milan, Italy
Architect	Giò Ponti
Structural Engineer	Pier-Luigi Nervi
Completion	1956
Height	127 m (416 ft)
Volume	ca 160 000 m³
Use	Offices in the tower; auditorium, canteen, conference rooms, etc. in the plinth

Urban context

The front of the tower faces the Piazza Duca d'Aosta as an architectural rival to Milan central station. Owing to its height, the Torre forms an impressive city landmark, visible from afar. The tower, which is set back from the piazza on the same plot, is enclosed by low buildings containing the office-tower installations and two bridges linked to the tower. Access to the main lobby is via an inclined drive. This aspect of the design makes the tower appear all the more impressive. Torre Pirelli used to be the head office of the tyre manufacturer from which it took its name. The building is now the seat of the regional administration of Lombardy.

Structure

The load-bearing structure – which has two triangules at each end, four central columns and two lift cores – tapers towards the top as the load decreases. The relatively thick floors taper towards the outside, to the advantage of the façade design. The impact of the load-bearing structure on the overall design betrays the masterful hand of Pier-Luigi Nervi, one of the best-known civil engineers in the 20th century.

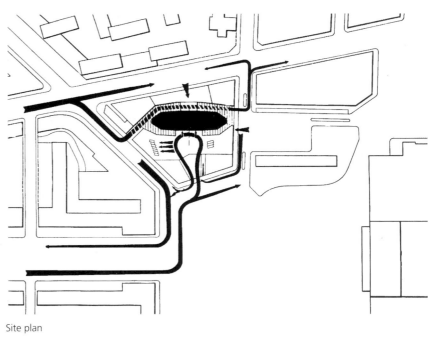

Site plan

Circulation / Installations

The main technical rooms for the building are located in the bottom floor. The vertical shafts rise through the triangles, each side of which has a lift and an emergency staircase. The two central shaft zones thus contain a total of six lifts which service every storey of the building.

Façade

The façade clearly reveals the tapering columns and solid triangles of the load-bearing structure. In order to balance the tapering columns and, at the same time, make the load-bearing structure stand out clearly against the façade, a vertical row of windows runs up the entire height of the building, becoming wider in inverse ratio to the tapering of the columns.

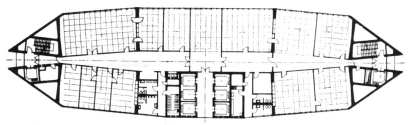

Upper floors

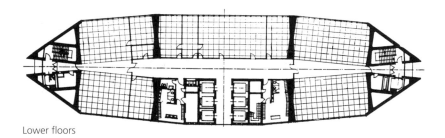

Lower floors

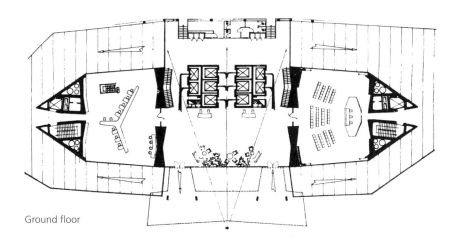

Ground floor

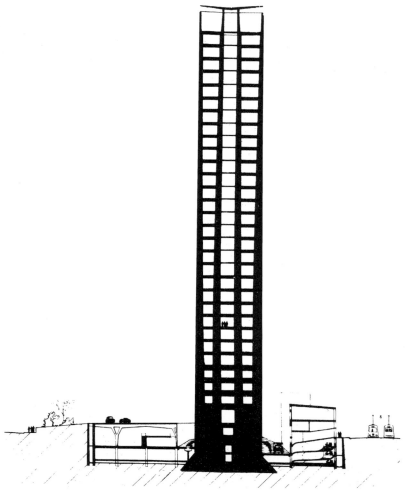

Structure section

THYSSENHAUS

Location	Düsseldorf, Germany
Architect	Hentrich / Petschnigg & Partners
Structural Engineer	Klöppel / Leonhardt
Completion	1957
Height	95 m (311 ft)
Volume	ca 140 000 m³
Use	Offices

Urban context

The area in and around Jan-Wellem Platz was considered ripe for development because the increase in population and motorised traffic called for new urban structures with green areas and large open spaces for the traffic. Urban planners in Düsseldorf were quick to recognise the inevitability of these developments. Plans to restructure the inner city thus focused on specific questions, such as that of constructing higher buildings to enhance the city skyline. When Phönix-Rheinrohr AG was looking for an impressive location in a city area in 1954, a competition was held for plans to construct a new tower. The design for the building, which consists of three flat slabs with the central one towering above the two offset on either side of it, was proposed by the prize-winning architects as the optimal solution, although it was not entered in the competition. The tower, which faces north-south, stands amidst the main streets as a trend-setting landmark. Together with the Düsseldorfer Hofgarten it forms a link between epochs and points of the compass.

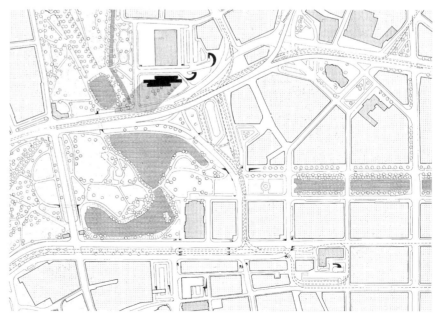

Site plan

Structure

The floor slabs rest on the clad columns, which are placed at rather regular intervals on the ground area. Each floor forms a coherent horizontal slab distributing the wind loads for the two horizontal and the two vertical steel framework braces. The reinforcing bracing is anchored in a 3-storey-high torsionally stiff foundation cellar.

Circulation / Installations

The core zone of the building is situated in the high central slab. Eight passenger lifts, a goods lift and two staircases, located in the vertical installation shafts, provide access to the offices; the ventilation and electricity shafts form the ends of the core zone. The technical installations are housed in the two basement floors and in the top three floors.

Façade

The long sides are clad with large, non-load-bearing curtain walls whose glass surfaces reflect the park landscape. The vertically articulated glass skin and the horizontal parapet elements are harmoniously balanced. The tripartite articulation of the short sides is accentuated by corrugated sheeting.

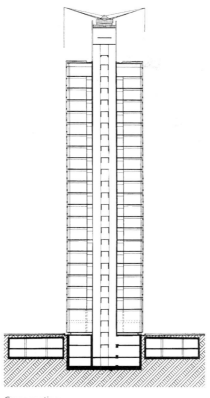

Cross section

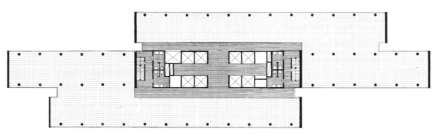

Typical storey

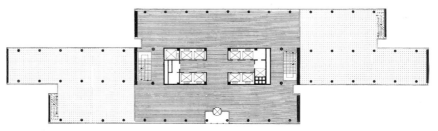

Ground floor

INLAND STEEL BUILDING

Location	Chicago, IL, USA
Architect	SOM Skidmore, Owings & Merrill
Structural Engineer	SOM
Completion	1958
Height	95 m (313 ft)
Volume	ca 97 000 m³
Use	Office

Urban context

The complex of buildings stands on a site 58.5 m x 36.5 m in the Loop district, Chicago's business quarter. Only 66% of the plot has been built on, so the building stands out clearly from the city blocks in the neighbourhood. The complex as a whole consists of a 19-storey office tower whose floors are entirely free of supporting pillars, and a 25-storey service tower housing all the secondary rooms, stairs, lifts and supply shafts. This division of functions in the structural organisation leads to an interesting tension between the part of the building being served and that providing services, between the open, glazed structure and the sealed, clad section.

Structure

Seven stainless-steel-clad outer columns are situated peripherally along the longitudinal sides of the building. The transverse girders freely span the entire 18-m depth of the building. The ceiling girders (which have apertures for the service lines and piping) and the cellular-steel floor are supported by the columns.

The floor area of the seventeen upper stories is based on a grid of 1.575 m x 1.575 m and can be subdivided with a specially developed system of prefabricated partition walls.

Circulation / Installations

The entire installations and vertical access are located in the separate service tower, from where connecting passages provide access to each of the storeys.

Façade

The exterior appearance is very much defined by the structure of the external columns and the curtain walls. In marked contrast with the smooth steel-plate cladding of the service tower, the frames and glazing bars are made of stainless steel, filled in with laminated glass and sheet steel plates. The plate arrangement corresponds to that of the laminated glass on the office block. Serving as a clear and simple metaphor, the outer appearance reveals the internal processes of a corporate steel group in the 20th century.

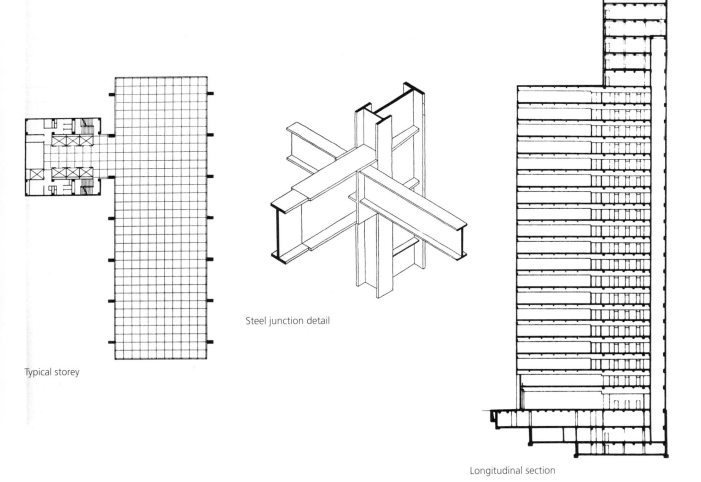

Typical storey

Steel junction detail

Longitudinal section

SEAGRAM BUILDING

Location	New York, NY, USA
Architect	L. Mies van der Rohe, Philip Johnson
Completion	1958
Height	157 m (515 ft)
Volume	490 000 m³
Use	Restaurant, office

Urban context

The 39-storey Seagram Building stands on Park Avenue in the centre of Manhattan's business district. Set back approximately twenty-seven meters from the street, the skyscraper rises above a surrounding terrace lining the main street and two side streets. Adopting a radically new approach to integrating a building into its urban environment, Mies van der Rohe positioned the Seagram skyscraper in the centre of the site instead of directly alongside Park Avenue.

The Seagram Building, which rests on a granite plinth, has a ceremonial entrance created by the two symmetrically arranged fountains. Thanks to this design, the building is a major landmark – both horizontally and vertically – on Park Avenue. Lewis Mumford was impressed that the building was visible from three sides and accessible to pedestrians, creating rather than occupying space. The building itself consists of two overlaid T-shaped volumes, whereby the lower part, hidden by the main structure, fills the entire site. Philip Johnson designed "The Four Seasons" restaurant and bar on the ground floor.

Structure

The Seagram Building is a steel skeleton structure. The offices have a clearance of nine feet (2.75 m) and an integrated support grid.

The space between the columns is divided into six window units with a distance of 28 ft (8.5 m) in each direction. In the offices, partition walls can be installed behind each window support.

Circulation / Installations

There are four lift shafts on the ground floor, arranged within the support grid (the shafts measure 12.7 m x 2.5 m). Each of the two central shafts contains six lifts, a secondary room, and a technical equipment shaft. The exterior shafts each contain three lifts, a secondary room, a technical equipment shaft and a staircase.

In the upper storeys, the four shafts, together with the sanitary rooms adjoined where required, make up the entire central infrastructure for the offices.

Façade

Above the 7-m-high ground floor, a curtain wall of brown-tinted solar glass and bronze encloses the building's steel skeleton construction. The visible use of bronze on the external skin lends the building its unique dignity. The following materials used for the ground floor: granite slabs for the floors and terrace, travertine slabs around the lift shafts, and bronze cladding on the columns.

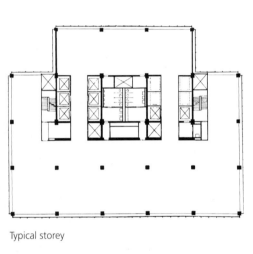

Typical storey

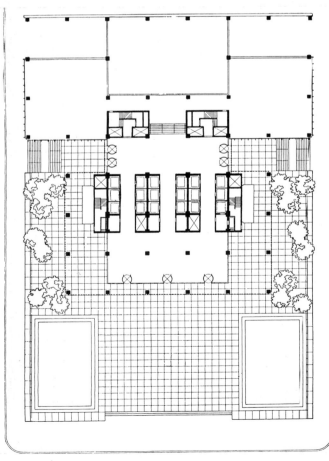

Ground floor

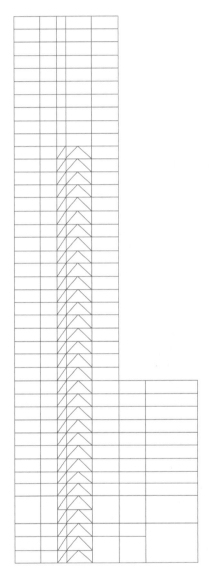

Structural grid

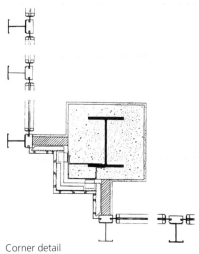

Corner detail

45

TORRE VELASCA

Location	Milan, Italy
Architects	BBPR Architects Banfi, Belgiojoso, Peressutti and Rogers
Structural Engineer	Arturo Danusso
Completion	1958
Height	99 m (325 ft)
Volume	84 000 m³
Use	Shops, offices, apartments

Urban context

The Torre Velasca stands in Milan city centre, in the midst of a dense network of streets. The building is surrounded by a block open at one side only. The tower has been designed accordingly: the broad side of the Torre has been extended at the ground and the first-floor levels and opens out to the square facing the street. A cross-section shows a further relationship to the neighbouring buildings, with the lower part of the structure maintaining a distance to the other buildings. In the upper section, where space permits, the structure has been extended. The widening of the upper section is founded in the architect's intention to revert to the traditional meaning of the city horizon – which, at one time, would have been achieved with bell-towers, towers and domes – by erecting a memorably designed tower in the rather monotonous cityscape of today. The Torre Velasca takes into account the particular urban situation at other levels too, as in the façade design (the size and positioning of the windows), the choice of materials and the arrangement of the building's functions.

Structure

The tower's load-bearing structure consists of a central core and peripheral columns, arranged at a distance of 8 m around the core. In this way, a flexible plan design has been achieved. The foundation is composed of a concrete bed that absorbs the forces. The technical installations are also located here.

In the broader section, the forces are absorbed and transferred by a special structure.

The wind forces are absorbed by the core alone.

Circulation / Installations

The core contains eight lifts and two staircases, all arranged symmetrically. Four of the lifts have been offset slightly and serve floors one to eight. Their positioning accentuates the direction in which the building is facing, whilst simultaneously creating greater circulation space. Two other lifts are assigned to the two staircases, which link all twenty-eight floors. All the shafts are located in the core area.

Façade

The façade design is determined by three basic elements: the visible load-bearing piers; the masonry in between, with apertures for windows and loggias; and a second structure with column-like elements subdividing the area between the large piers. The traditional form of the windows (positioned at regular intervals in the office section and arranged more casually in the section above) establishes a relationship with the neighbouring buildings.

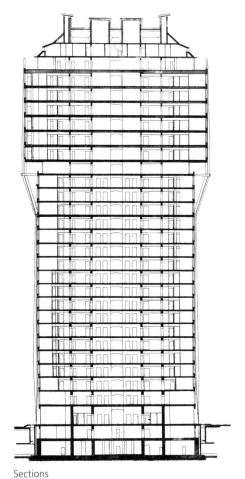
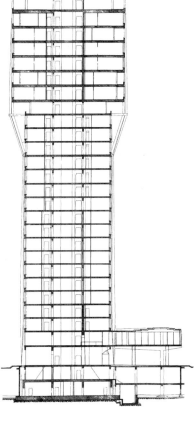

Sections

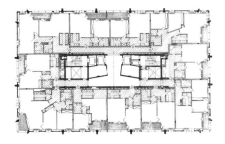

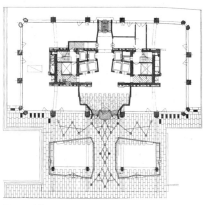

Ground floor

UNION CARBIDE BUILDING

Location	New York, NY, USA
Architect	SOM Skidmore, Owings & Merrill
Structural Engineer	SOM
Completion	1960
Height	212 m (696 ft)
Volume	ca 560 000 m³
Use	Office

Urban context

Located between Park Ave. and Vanderbilt Ave., the Union Carbide Building, with its 52-storey tower, constitutes a central focus for the surrounding city district. The bordering street space extends into the open ground floor of the building. The lack of a prestigious entrance suggests the public character of the area beneath the tower, which is clearly set back from the edges of the site. This, combined with the decision to position the load-bearing structure so that it projects from the corners of the building, creates an effect of tactful and almost self-confident elegance. The site generates a sense of great suspense, intensified at night by conspicuous illuminated ceilings which seem to make the building float mysteriously. Its sphere of influence creates a space directing the flow of pedestrians towards Grand Central Station. The expectation that one can enter the building axially through the lift core, which penetrates the street area, is countered by the metal letters UNION CARBIDE. Instead, two inconspicuous glass doors to the right and left lead to two identically shaped draft lobbies, via which, after several changes of direction, one arrives in the cool, elegant lobby on the first floor. It is here that one first enters the building proper. The desired publicity value of the ensemble lies in the masterly and subtle negation of its vast dimensions, which are nevertheless ever-present; the tower dominates the street space without infringing upon it. The impression of power becomes all the more

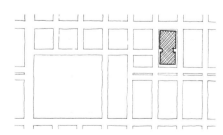

Site plan

insistent due to the subliminal staging of the whole; it is not apparent in the insignia, in a chic lobby or a in a presitigious drive, but rather in the self-evident absence of such symbols.

Structure

A relatively simple steel frame structure was designed, typical of the then prevailing economic approach to solving structural problems. However, when it came to the façade cladding, exemplary and complex structural solutions were found for the load transfer, wind resistance, weatherproofing, insulation, glare-proofing and external appearance of the building. The SOM architects were subsequently viewed as *the* skyscraper builders in the USA, which they demonstrated most impressivley with the John Hancock Center and Sears Tower.

Circulation / Installations

The Union Carbide Buidling is renowned for its novel integrated illumination, air-conditioning and sound control systems. These units are completely hidden between the ceiling proper and the counter ceiling, which consists of a grid of metal sections, perforated to promote ventilation, and inlaid translucent plastic panels creating the illuminated ceiling. Neither lighting, loudspeakers nor microphones are visible. In this way, the internal spaces assume a totally abstract character – technical necessities appear not to exist, and not even the source of lighting can be localised. A low-key system of perfect control.

Façade

As in the case of the Seagram Building, which served as its model, the façade of the steel skeleton structure has been developed logically from the inner structure and, indeed, becomes its image. In front of the very prominent columns and floor ends, a system of glass surfaces has been constructed, secured in strong, aluminium mullions. Solar protection is provided by interior, vertical, narrow sunbreakers.

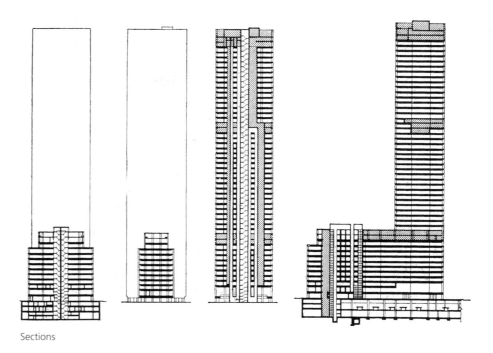

Sections

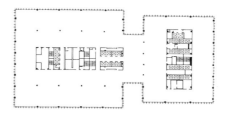

Typical storeys

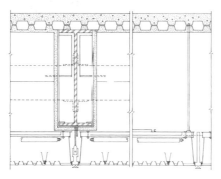

Façade detail

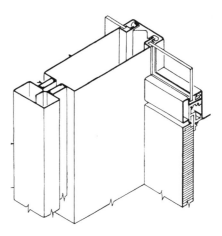

CHASE MANHATTAN BANK

Location	New York, NY, USA
Architect	SOM Skidmore, Owings & Merrill
Structural Engineer	SOM with Weiskopf & Pickworth
Completion	1961
Height	245 m (813 ft)
Volume	ca 700 000 m³
Use	Bank, Office

Urban context

Seen against the New York skyline of 1961, the rectangular building of the Chase Manhattan Bank distinguishes itself radically from the skyscrapers erected earlier. The enormous building stands out not so much due to its height as its volume. Whereas the older skyscrapers tapered in cigar-like fashion towards the crown, the top of the 60-storey Chase Manhattan Bank tower is wide and sturdy, standing there like a drawer pulled out vertically amidst the haphazardly soaring older skyscrapers. As with the Union Carbide Building, designed by the same architects, the developers were not interested in building over the entire plot. Although the plot is amongst the most expensive in New York, almost seventy per cent of the 2.5-acre plot was designed as a public plaza.

The Chase Corporation's decision not to move to uptown Park Avenue but to "stay at home" with the new structure, triggered a chain reaction of reconstruction and new building as well as a process of reinvigoration within the banking district that continues to this day.

Structure

The rectangular tower, with a side-to-side ratio of 1:3, is composed of a steel structure with interior supports grouped around the core zone, and external piers rising in front of the façades. The 8.7-m primary structure is composed of six standardised modules of 1.45 m each. On the narrow sides, the load-bearing supports have been placed on the interior, so that the load-supporting structure seems to be formed by the ten huge frames. To prevent the steel skeleton from expanding excessively due to temperature changes, the piers on the thirty uppermost floors were insulated with hard foamed glass. Difficulties also presented themselves in joining the horizontal floor girders to the façade piers, as it was not possible to use cross-bracing. To overcome this problem, the horizontal girders were doubled and reinforced by plates welded onto the top edge. The floor-bearing beams are ninety centimetres high and provided with recesses for the piping.

Circulation / Installations

The core zone located in the centre of the building consists of thirty-eight lifts, the emergency stairs, shafts and technical rooms. The lower thirty floors are used as offices by the Chase Manhattan Bank, thus necessitating a different circulation system from the 31st floor upwards.

Façade

The principle of using a curtain wall as a façade had already been highly developed when it came to deciding whether to clad the skeleton with anodised aluminium or stainless steel. Although both materials would have met the demands of surface impression, cost and efficiency, the decision was finally made to use aluminium, because the supplier offered a much longer guarantee. The black aluminium sheeting cladding is visible on all sides. On the long sides, additional vertical pier cladding has been used to provide a contrast to the narrow, light aluminium profiles rising to the top of the building.

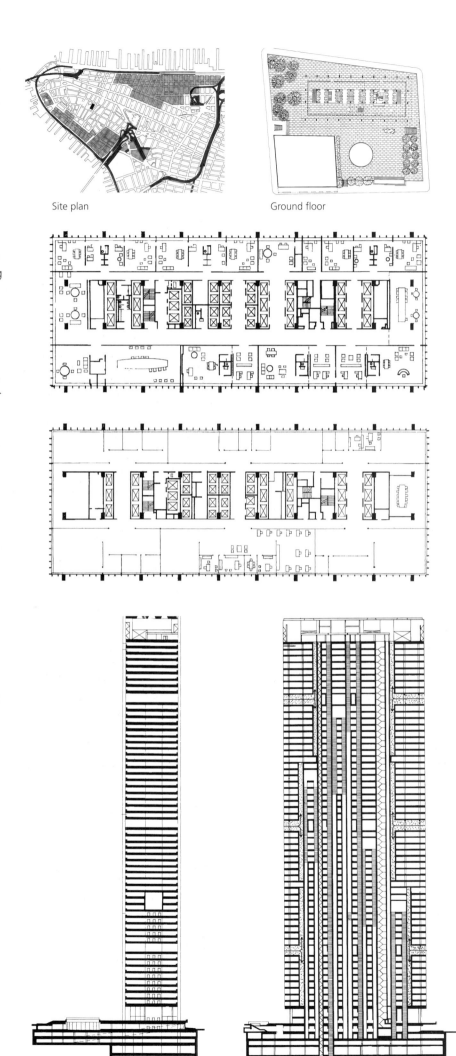

Site plan

Ground floor

Sections

METLIFE BUILDING

Location	New York, NY, USA
Architect	Walter Gropius, Emery Roth & Sons, and Pietro Belluschi
Structural Engineer	The Office of J. Ruderman
Completion	1963
Height	246 m (808 ft)
Volume	ca 890 000 m³
Use	Office, stores, restaurants

Urban context

The building, which formerly belonged to Pan Am, stands in the heart of Manhattan's East Side on the axis of Park Avenue between the New York General Building and the terminal of Grand Central Station. Having a direct connection to the underground station complex, the 59-storey building stands at what used to be one of the busiest locations in the world. The entrance hall at street level provides access both to Grand Central Station and to the lobby floor. The 49-storey tower rises from a 10-storey plinth built against the station concourse of the same height. The building profits from its unique location in the urban landscape, marked by the underground railway line and Grand Central Station. The offices are much sought after because of their spectacular view over Park Avenue and 44th Street. Only three months after the building opened, over 90% of the building's floor space of some 225 000 m³ was already leased.

Structure

The building is a steel skeleton structure with a reinforcing core. The columns are made from steel girders cased in concrete. The tower and the plinth form two separate static systems, each with its own foundations.

Circulation / Installations

Thousands of people use the building during daytime. Sixty-four lifts are designed to ensure a maximum waiting time of twelve seconds.

As the building was constructed directly over the tracks of the railway station, it has no basement as such. The air-conditioning system therefore had to be installed at a height of 225 m.

Façade

The façade of both tower and base consists of prefabricated concrete components with a quartz admixture. Marble, granite and bronze were used for the façades at street level. The vertical piers, which project 35 cm from the otherwise flush surface, give the building a ribbed effect. The loggia floors on the 21st and 46th storeys, with large panes of glass in aluminium frames, divide the façade into three sections. According to Walter Gropius, the tower's prismatic ground plan provided recessing for the centrally located lifts and ensured elegance of design.

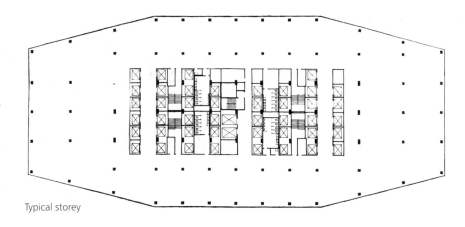

Typical storey

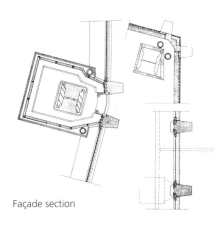

Façade section

Model

THE ECONOMIST BUILDING

Location	London, Great Britain
Architect	Alison and Peter Smithson
Structural Engineer	Sir Robert McAlpine & Sons
Completion	1965
Height	ca 65 m
Volume	ca 40 000 m³
Use	Office

Urban context

The preconditions for the construction of the new Economist Group building were laid during the War. After a number of moves, the publisher bought a 5-storey building near St. James's Street in the heart of London. The project for a new publishing house was launched by Sir Geoffrey Crowther at the end of the 1950s. Crowther insisted that the responsible project manager, Peter Dallas-Smith, comply with two conditions: firstly, that he entrust the execution of the project to a building contractor with whom the publisher had cordial relations and, secondly, that an apartment be located on the top of the new tower, which was to be at least ten storeys high. This second demand had a decisive influence on the development of the project. In order to satisfy the zoning laws, the publisher had to acquire almost 10 000 square metres of additional floor space in the vicinity, which it succeeded in doing thanks to Dallas-Smith's negotiating skills. The Economist Group partly owes its present prosperity to this circumstance, since land prices have risen considerably in the meantime. An interview competition was held to find an architect. The pro-avant-garde husband-and-wife team, the Smithsons, convinced the owners with their proposal for a mixed composition instead of a single tower. The final version provided for a lower bank building along the street front to St. James's Street. The 17-storey Economist Tower was thereby pushed back to the rear

of the site. The almost quadratic plot was completed by the existing Boodles Club and a third block. By giving the bank building a diagonal inner façade, the architects created what was probably the most exciting square in London, a square that lived from the interplay of diverse dimensions, the corresponding asymmetry, the uniform boundaries and the contrast of old and new, of constraining and open space.

Structure

A reinforcing core of concrete on the interior permits a clear-span zone extending to the perimeter, where the façade columns transfer the loads to the ground. Despite the great variety of uses, i.e. apartments, rooms, offices, control centres, all of the buildings in the ensemble display the same structural features. The Economist Tower and the smaller Resident Tower are almost entirely lined by arcades on the ground floor.

Circulation / Installations

Moving the vertical access links, which (in Great Britain) had traditionally been situated behind a ventilated façade, into the very interior of the building was a novelty at the time. A compact and economical core, inspired by American examples, contains the main elements of the infrastructure.

Façade

The Economist ensemble resembles a monotonous, prefabricated urban factory. However, its urbane impact lies in the skilled balanced attained with simple, repetitive motifs and the seemingly self-evident use of compaction, the variety of outer space as well as the contrasts which – together with the consistent treatment of the stone and glass composition – lend the whole ensemble a familiar air.

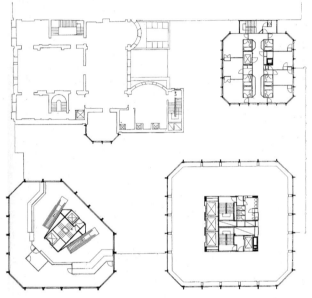

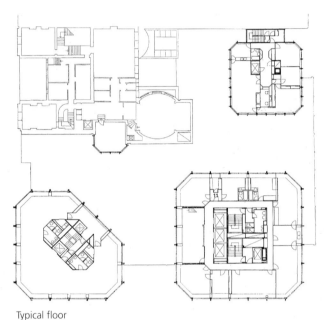

1st floor

Typical floor

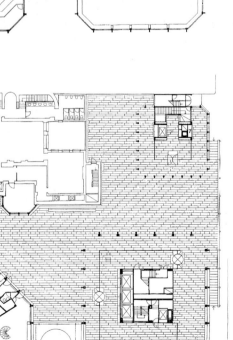

Ground floor

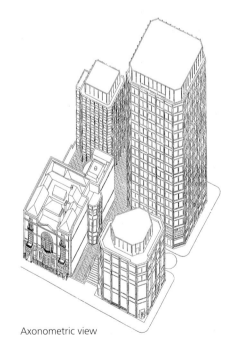

Axonometric view

MARINA CITY

Location	Chicago, IL, USA
Architect	Bertrand Goldberg Associates
Structural Engineer	Severud, Perrone, Fischer, Sturm, Conlin, Bandel
Completion	1962
Height	179 m (588 ft)
Volume	ca 350 000 m³
Use	Residential, office

Urban context

Marina City stands directly next to the Chicago River. It consists of a sunken base element for public use – providing access to the river and the boat mooring facilities – two residential towers and an office building, which forms the spatial boundary of the complex. The two circular towers are slightly offset. In this way, they avoid using the strict grid pattern and simultaneously allow an open view to the river. Marina City was initially the first mixed-use center city complex in the United States to include residential apartments. With 896 apartments, it is also the most densely inhabited building complex in Chicago, yet despite its density it does not lose any of its light and translucent character.

The exterior form is to be interpreted as Goldberg's critique of the prevalent contemporary block skyscraper. The organic form he has chosen represents a revolt against an era of static space, straight-lined contours, and a vision of humankind understood in terms of the machine.

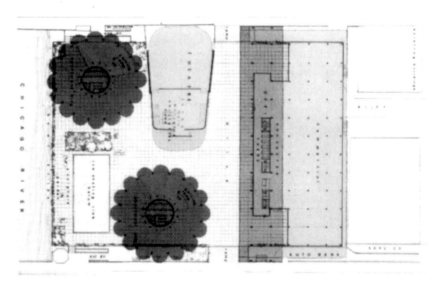

Site plan

Structure

The liberating form of the 65-storey "twin corn cobs" is borne by homogeneous reinforced steel structures. The tube-like lift shaft – the inner spine of the building – allows maximum use of the structural qualities of reinforced concrete. From the supports around the inner core, lamella-shaped segmental arches stretch to the outer supports of the structure. Such a circular skeleton structure, ensuring better streamlining, allows considerable savings on materials. Thus, each tower cost 10% less than it would have done using a standard construction.

Circulation / Installations

In this radially structured building, the tube-shaped core zone lies in the centre of the circular ground plan. The core contains five lifts and an emergency stairwell. The exits needed to be positioned differently on each storey to stabilise the building, thus making two alternately used core floor plans necessary.

Façade

The semicircular balcony elements define the exterior border of the façade and make the interior structure recognisable from outside. The glass inner skin serves as a climatic shield, although transparency is considerably restricted by some of the installations. The reinforced concrete structure dominates the entire complex and, at first glance, makes the towers appear unfinished, as if awaiting completion. This impression is reinforced by the 20-storey-high ramp construction of the parking area. Nevertheless, with their external form reduced to a basic structural principle, the two towers reveal a highly radical approach in skyscraper construction. In 1965, the building was awarded a silver medal by the Architectural League of New York.

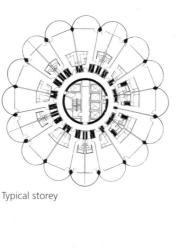

Typical storey

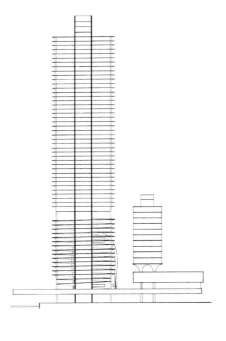

TORRES BLANCAS

Location	Madrid, Spain
Architect	J. Saenz de Oiza
Structural Engineer	F. Casado y J. Manterda
Completion	1968
Height	72 m (236 ft)
Volume	ca 80 000 m³
Use	Apartments, services

Urban context

The original project provided for three residential towers constructed by the exit road – on the outskirts of Madrid – to the airport in the direction of Barcelona. These three towers were intended to lend the area an urban character. Their urban quality was, in fact, already contained in their mixed use, which was defined vertically: the entrance area on the ground floor, residential and service areas in the middle section, and social amenities – a restaurant, a bar and a swimming pool – on the upper floors. Although only one of the towers was completed, it made an important contribution to a period in which organic tendencies were current in Spanish architecture.

Structure

The load-bearing structure is composed of horizontal discs borne by huge columns containing, among other things, the sewage water pipes. The building is reinforced by continuous rows of vertical slabs, which perform a load-bearing function.

Circulation / Installations

The lifts are located centrally. The rooms have natural through ventilation. The installations, which are tailored to meet the needs of the occupants, are comparatively modest.

Site sketch

Façade

The basic idea behind the tower was to create a "vertical garden city". The appearance of the shell was preserved after completion, since none of the window elements are visible. They are well set back from the undulating façade and remain invisible from the outside, being concealed in the shadows cast by the large, rounded cantilevered balconies. Considering the extreme climatic conditions in Madrid, this is quite a favourable solution, since it ensures sufficient shade in the summer whilst shielding users from the cold winds in the winter.

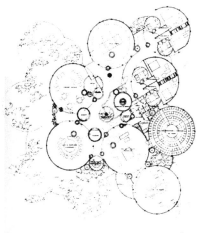

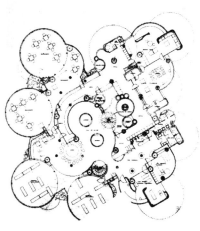

Floor plans

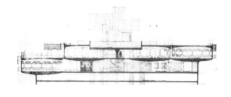

CBS BUILDING

Location	New York, NY, USA
Architect	Eero Saarinen
Completion	1965
Height	150 m (491 ft)
Volume	ca 225 000 m³
Use	Office

Urban context

In the 1960s, upper Manhattan experienced far-reaching transformations, especially around 6th Avenue. The relatively cheap, rather dilapidated residential area became a fashionable business district with hotels and administrative buildings. Located in the centre of this district, the CBS Building is surrounded by a narrow square that follows the line of the street.

Structure

The supporting structure consists of a circle of concrete pillars around the perimeter of the building and a central core, also made of concrete. Saarinen followed Sullivan (the influential architect of early skyscrapers) in his view that the logical relation between the parts creates movement, which, in turn, generates a sense of the vertical. Saarinen once remarked, when referring to the building's form, that "The sense of vertical in the tower is underlined by the relief created by the triangular pillars between the windows. They start at ground-level and rise 491 feet."

The core contains the sanitation and service zone, vertical access via lifts and emergency stairways, and supply shafts. This provides ample open space for offices between the well-defined load-bearing structure consisting of the pillars (the outer shell) and the core (the centre). The load-bearing structure is maintained from ground floor through to the top floor.

Circulation / Installations

The building has two main technical areas, one over the lobby and the other on the top floor, both servicing the office space in between. Access is provided by a total of sixteen lifts (and two emergency staircases) with eight lifts each for floors 1-21 and floors 21-38.

Façade

This imposing, solid 38-storey building is characterised by the cubic, facetted grey pillars, which divide the façade into narrow compartments and run from the base to the top of the sky-scraper. The triangular parallel supports of roughened anthracite-coloured marble slabs lend the building an abstract quality, simultaneously elegant and sombre, which, intensified by the sharp contours of light and shadow, make the "black cliff" appear higher than it really is. The pillar grid, which determines the width of the entrances, is not interrupted at the main entrance area. The concrete pillars form a relief that constantly changes as one moves around the building.

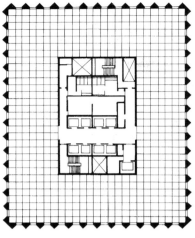

Office storey

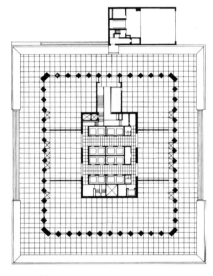

Ground floor

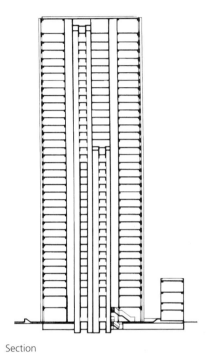

Section

CIVIC CENTER

Location	Chicago, IL, USA
Architect	C.F. Murphy Associates; Skidmore Owings & Merrill; and Loebl, Schlossmann and Bennett
Structural Engineer	SOM
Completion	1965
Height	194 m (635 ft)
Volume	ca 650 000 m³
Use	Office, courtrooms

Urban context

The 31-storey Chicago Civic Center lies on the Dearborn Corridor, an area the city acquired in order either to sell to financially strong investors or to use for public projects. Along the same road, there are a number of banks, the Marina Towers, and other buildings. The Chicago Civic Center has now been renamed the Richard J. Daley Center, after the man who served for many years as mayor of the city.
The block is set at right-angles to the street so that, together with the Brunswick Office Building (another SOM project), an open plaza is created which is often used for official ceremonies and spontaneous demonstrations.

Structure

The tower is divided into nine sections giving it span widths of ca. 26.5 m x 14 m (87 ft x 47 ft) – most unusual for skyscrapers. This design required welded steel braced girders of 160 cm in height supporting a 17cm-thick concrete floor, which transfers the forces of the wind into the centre. The edge roof beams are set in concrete, with steel plates from self-oxidising Cor-Ten steel serving simultaneously as form, façade cladding and reinforcement. For this purpose, seamless welding was used on the whole façade. In the workshops, the steel supports, with a cross-shaped cross section, were welded from steel plates into two-storey units. All the joints were welded on

the construction site. The support section of 152 cm on the ground floor tapers gradually to 61 cm towards the top of the tower.

Cor-Ten steel was developed in 1933 in the USA to prevent the extreme corrosion which rail cars are exposed to. It was first used to produce load-bearing supports in the John Deere Building in Moline, designed by the architect Eero Saarinen, and finished in 1964.

Circulation / Installations

The cores of the tower taper towards the top, thus limiting their static function. For this reason, not all of the thirty-six lifts on the ground floor actually serve the very top floors. The core also contains two emergency staircases and the sanitary facilities. Horizontal shafts run through the whole building in the core and are led between the steel load-bearing floor supports to the courtrooms, which are in part sealed units.

Façade

Special emphasis has been given to two sections of the grid façade: the 9th and 10th storeys, marked by horizontal segments, and the parapet area, which are characterised by the absence of horizontal articulation. These accentuated areas each mark a double-storey section of courtrooms. The Civic Center façade consists entirely of oxidised Cor-Ten steel and bronze-tinted glass. This cladding is not only designed to serve the purpose of weather protection, but also serves to reinforce the steel plates. A Picasso sculpture in the same Cor-Ten steel can be seen on Daley Place. Together with the façade, it forms an appealing urban ensemble.

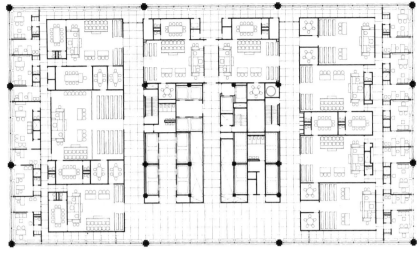

Court storey

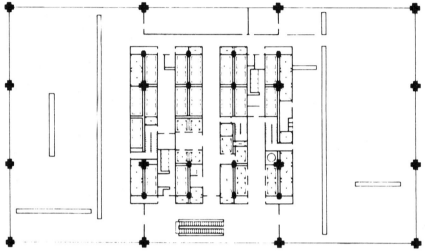

Public storey

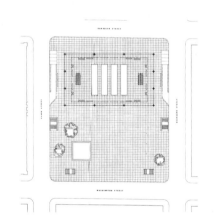

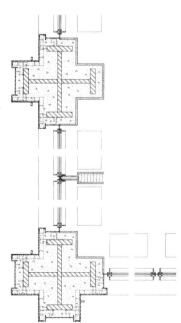

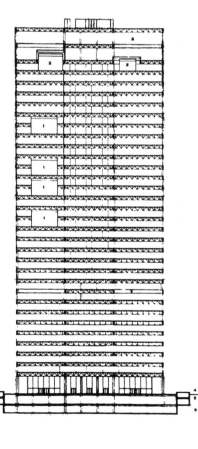

KNIGHTS OF COLUMBUS

Location	New Haven, CT, USA
Architect	Kevin Roche / John Dinkeloo & Associates
Completion	1965
Height	71 m (233 ft)
Volume	ca 45 000 m³
Use	Services, office

Urban context

This complex, with an administration building and a car park, is situated on one of the main entrance roads on the periphery of New Haven. Despite their joint, central access, both structures – planned at different – times, function completely independently of each other.

The compact impression made by the building stems from the structural requirements imposed by the high water table, because of which the car park was made to float above the ground like foreign body. The 23-storey administration building, with its abstract construction principle, contributes to this bizarre impression, in which all sense of proportion appears to be distorted.

Structure

During the first stage of construction, the four corner towers were completely finished before the main girders of the twenty-three storeys to the central lift tower were installed in a second phase. All the metal girders are made of corrosion-resistant untreated steel. Dark brown, glazed tiles were used to clad the concrete surfaces.

Circulation / Installations

The six lifts are situated at the centre of the building, thus allowing flexible use of floor space. The building's main utilities are supplied via the four towers and serve the interior via intercostal girders.

The towers also contain the sanitary installations and the emergency stairs.

Façade

The distribution of the façade is determined by the arrangement of the intercostal girders. The radiators, which form a parapet, provide additional horizontal structure alongside the unclad primary girders. The cantilevered intercostal girders, which constitute the main sun shield, are augmented by adjustable blinds. All of the steel girders are visible from the outside, the corner towers alone being clad with tiles.

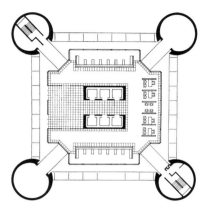
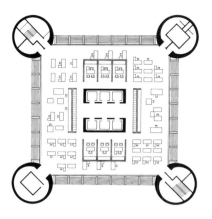

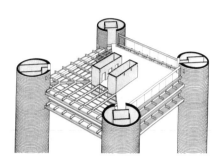

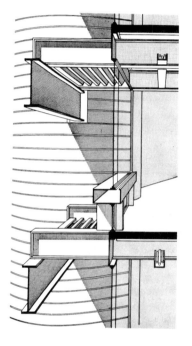

PLACE VICTORIA OFFICE TOWERS

Location	Montreal, Canada
Architect	Luigi Moretti
Structural Engineer	P.L. Nervi
Completion	1966
Height	185 m (606 ft)
Volume	380 000 m³
Use	Stock exchange, office, restaurants, shops

Urban context

Located between the commercial and financial districts, the complex acts as a kind of interface. Its original design as a twin tower made the building complex and an unmistakable landmark; and the two towers formed a point of reference for the surrounding areas. However, only one was built. The main entrance and vertical access lie on the longitudinal axis of the complex; there are side access points between the middle building and the towers, creating an orthogonal, urban-like access structure. The points of intersection thus created constitute the vertical links between the entrance level and the public basement. The size and form of the access area, which has been raised by a number of steps, defines the side providing main access in the narrow wall facing the square.

Structure

The entire building is a reinforced concrete structure with a separate load-bearing structure for the middle section.

The towers have a centrally organised structure, whose four inner pillars and diagonal walls form the core. This core also links all twelve stories by means of girders (diagonal to the specially designed corner pillars) extending over two stories. Corresponding to their load, the girders and corner pillars taper towards the top of the building. The floors are also monolithically linked to the structure.

Circulation / Installations

The heating and air-conditioning are organised in sections. The installations are housed in the roof areas of the towers, in the middle section and in each of two mezzanines developed from the load-bearing structure. In addition to the sanitation, the core of the tower contains two stairwells and ten of the building's twenty-two lifts. The other twelve are arranged around the core. Towards the top of the tower, the number of lifts decreases by six per section.

Façade

The entire complex has uniform glass curtain-wall façades on all sides. The four corner pillars are positioned to reflect the cross-shaped structure of the ground plan so that the diagonal structure is visible from the outside. Together with its slightly convex form, this gives the façade the appearance of taut skin, which is interrupted at the equipment floors. Here again, the inner structure is visible, defining the building on the vertical plane, too.

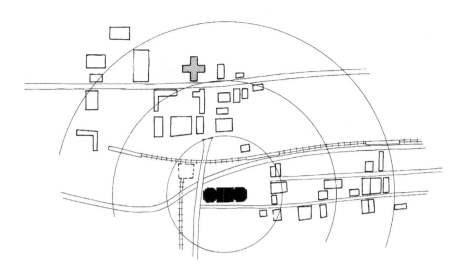

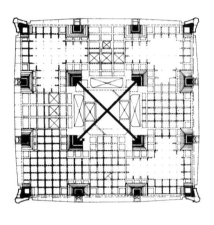

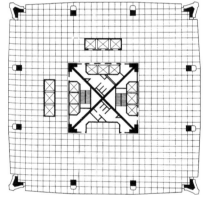

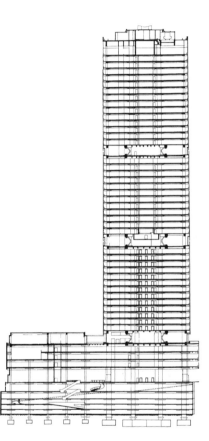

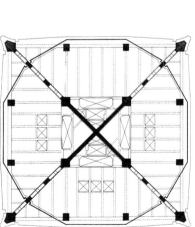

AUSTRALIA SQUARE

Location	Sidney, Australia
Architect	Harry Seidler & Associates
Completion	1967
Height	183 m (600 ft)
Volume	ca 241 000 m³
Use	Services, office

Urban context

Australia Square, which occupies an area of approximately 4 000 square metres in the centre of Sidney, unites two office buildings grouped around a spacious pedestrian zone. The partially planted lower pedestrian level passes below the 13-storey office building – which stands on piles – from Pitt Street and gives pedestrians an opportunity to rest in the cafés and on the recessed seats. This zone opens up into the Shopping Circle. From the lower level, stairs take pedestrians to the upper level raised a few steps above Bond Street, the main shopping street. This level has been made into the prestigious platform of the cylindrical 46-storey tower, which contains rentable office space on the first floor, an exhibition area, and a restaurant on the two upper floors. The transparent ground floor, a continuation of the surrounding platform, merely serves as a front zone for the outward-facing lifts. In the words of Harry Seidler: "The essence of a high-rise building is vertical transport. It is the way to get in and therefore the lifts must be obvious."

Australia Square is one of a number of set-back buildings dating from this period in which the desire to bring more light and air into Sidney's densely built-up city centre was given priority over prestigious appearance. The arrangement of the building elements and surfaces is open to a variety of interpretations. Although there are undoubtedly functional reasons for the form and location of the tower, it is equally possible that Harry Seidler drew his inspiration from closely studying the tracts of classical architecture.

Like Alberti's ideal church, the tower is white; it stands in the centre of a rectangular area, imposing a radial form on the floor design. The building proper is surrounded by a colonnade, whilst the exposed character of the ground floor manifests itself in an expressively curved rib-structure. Although Harry Seidler fulfils all the demands placed on modern and functional city and architectural planning, he nevertheless follows classical composition in his arrangement of the forms employed. Consequently, Australia Square is an initial expression of the discourse on post-modernism that is now beginning.

Structure

The form and organisation of the tower, which has a diameter of 42 m, called for a tube-in-tube structure. For the ceilings of the ground and first floors, which have to carry a greater part of the load, the engineer, Pier Luigi Nervi, adopted a system of curved concrete ribs, which meant correspondingly lower ceilings, whilst radial girders joined to the façade piers were employed on the higher floors. The pier depth diminishes towards the top of the building as the static load declines.

Circulation / Installations

The radial girders on the office floors allow for a flexible arrangement of both the lighting and the installation of the power connection lines. The air is conditioned via an external zone and an inner zone with high and low ventilation speeds respectively. Of the eighteen lifts serving the tower, five are arranged in three distinct groups of floors. Two lifts ascend to the restaurant on the top floors.

Façade

The twenty protruding concrete piers running the entire height of the building determine its outward appearance. Variety is provided by the interplay of light and dark vaulted areas provided by the parapet slabs and the glass fields between the piers.
Given rhythm by the set-back equipment storeys, the repetitive stacking terminates in a superelevated crown which, together with the open plinth area, reflects the principles of classical composition mentioned above.

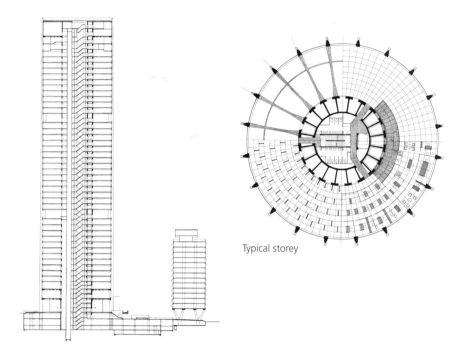

Typical storey

Ground floor

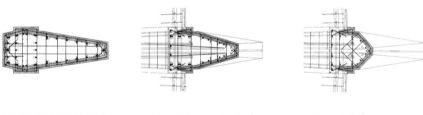

ALCOA BUILDING

Location	San Francisco, CA, USA
Architect	SOM Skidmore, Owings & Merrill
Structural Engineer	SOM
Completed	1968
Height	116 m (380 ft)
Volume	ca 215 000 m³
Use	Office

Urban structure

The Alcoa Building (now known as the Golden Gate Office Building) is situated in a newly developed residential and commercial district not far from the harbour. It stands near a 25-storey apartment block. SOM wanted to create a building whose strict forms and dominant appearance made it stand out clearly from the existing towers, thus reducing them visually to the scale of residential blocks. The building rises up above a 3-storey, publicly used garage designed by the architects Wurster, Bernardi & Emmons. As the substructure is relatively small, it does not really function as a base, so that the building loses contact with the ground and forfeits its dominance.

Structure

As the building stands in an earthquake area, the load-bearing structure was designed to absorb any seismic tremors. The load-bearing structure combines the advantages of bracing trusses, which are relatively rigid and keep lateral and other vibrations to a minimum and the moment-stayed outer steel cage, which is capable of absorbing severe earthquake tremors due to its great flexibility. In contrast to customary earthquake-proof structures, this combination increases resistance without causing any additional material costs.

Circulation / Installations

The centre of the building consists of a solid core containing three lifts, two staircases, the sanitation and the entire air-conditioning system.

Façade

The façade design is determined by the load-bearing structure, whose vertical columns and diagonal bracing recall the lattice girders of the Golden Gate Bridge piers. The curtain wall, which encloses the space, is located 46 cm behind the load-bearing structure. The cladding of the steel structure and the profiles of the curtain wall are made of bronze-coloured anodised aluminium. The spandrels are the same colour as the tinted glass windows

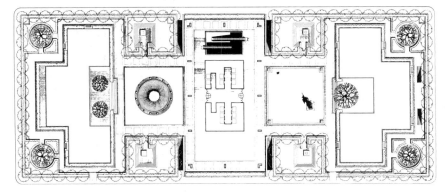

Ground floor

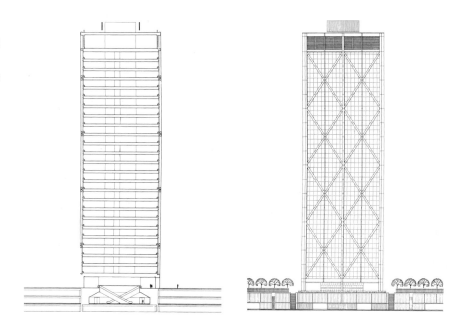

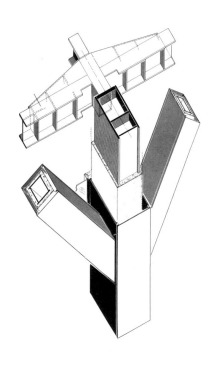

Structure junction

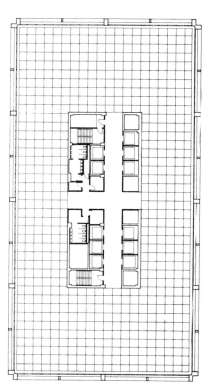

Typical storey

LAKE POINT TOWER

Location	Chicago, IL, USA
Architect	Schipporeit – Heinrich Associates with Graham, Anderson, Probst and White
Completion	1968
Height	197 m (646 ft)
Volume	ca 200 000 m³
Use	Residential, commercial, businesses, restaurants, swimming pool, fitness club

Urban context

Lake Point Tower stands alone in splendid isolation on a headland projecting into Lake Michigan, its elegant curved glass façade reflecting the light and the sky.

The whole plot is occupied by a 9.5-m-high base with various leisure facilities on the roof, including a naturally landscaped park, which seeks to establish a balance between the urban environment and the lake. Plans for two further similarly shaped towers were never realised. The point of reference for the 65-storied, clover-leaf shaped, reinforced concrete tower was the 1922 Mies van der Rohe design for a completely transparent office tower. However, it was impossible to apply van der Rohe's idea of a translucent skyscraper to an apartment block with 900 flats; such a notion may well only come into question for a truly "transparent administration". But despite all of these shortcomings, Lake Point Tower remains a prismatic structure of great expressive force and daring. Its wave-shaped curves and almost abstract glass surfaces make it a worthy tribute to the genius of Mies van der Rohe and his ability to make what was actually difficult appear extremely simple.

Structure

The horizontal forces are transferred through the triangular central core, which together with the façade supports, runs through the whole height of the building. The curtain-wall façade itself is not a load-bearing structure.

Circulation / Installations

Supply shafts have been so laid out within each apartment that the size of each apartment can be changed according to the prevailing market demands. Main access is via the triangular central core, which has nine lifts, three staircases, the service shafts and express supply corridors. Lake Point Tower does not have centralised air-conditioning control; each apartment has its own separate heating and air-conditioning units. Fresh air can be regulated manually via the façade.

Façade

The bronze-tinted elevation consists of a curved glass curtain-wall. The greatest possible amount of privacy is ensured through the 120-degree angle of the ground plan, which makes it impossible for the neighbours to look into the next-door apartment. Integrated air-supply units for manual use mark the separate storeys and follow the horizontal division of the façade. Since skyscrapers rarely stand alone, they are rarely seen in their totality – and certainly never from as many different perspectives as Lake Point Tower.

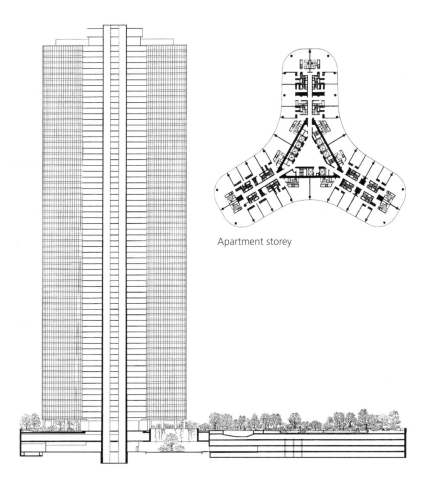

Apartment storey

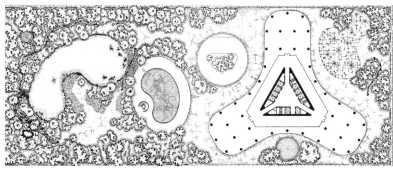

Site plan

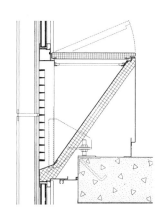

ONE FIRST NATIONAL PLAZA

Location	Chicago, IL, USA
Architect	C.F. Murphy Associates with Perkins & Will
Structural Engineer	C.F. Murphy Associates
Completion	1969
Height	259 m (850 ft)
Volume	ca 800 000 m³
Use	Office

Urban context

The 60-storey building for the One First National Bank of Chicago headquarters triggered the development boom in Chicago's inner city. The design team developed an office skyscraper consisting of a single, 60-storey tapering curve. This design was born out of the need for large, unimpeded circulation areas providing public access on the lower floors, and, on the upper floors, smaller areas for offices with natural lighting. The building, which stands perpendicular to the main streets, has a 2-storey atrium hall at street level. It is entered on the narrow ends through revolving doors (commonly used in American skyscrapers to exclude draughts) located at both sides of the circulation core.

A sunken courtyard at the front of one of the long sides provides a focus for activities around Dearborn Street, attracting office workers, tourists and shoppers throughout the day. Fountains and landscaping, and a major work by Marc Chagall – a massive rectangular mosaic – enhance this pleasant, public plaza in the Loop district. Its almost full capacity utilisation clearly demonstrates that both the choice of location and the uses offered have been a great success.

Structure

Corrugated steel sheeting covered with poured concrete resting on a steel girder grid provides a stable floor. This, in turn, lies on long prestressed steel-girders running from the outer to the inner supports. The construction method employed follows the Chicago tradition of using open, unimpeded space and ensures flexible use.

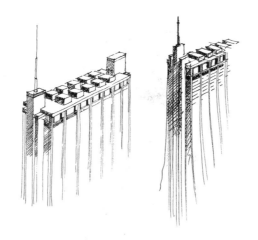

Circulation / Installations

The cores (located on the narrow sides) contain more than fifty lifts, the emergency stairs and installation shafts. Originally, the client had not wanted the cores to be constructed in the exterior façades, since he was endeavouring to provide the greatest possible utilisation of rentable space. However, this measure can be justified by the skyscraper's tapered form and the successful utilisation of the plot.

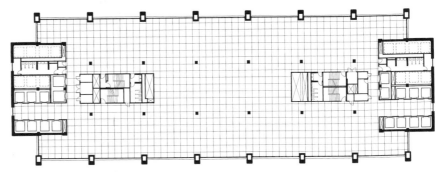

Typical storey

Façade

The façade is defined by the vertical piers, appearing to run down the building like cables. The horizontal bands, clad in the light Texan "Pearl Gray" granite contrast sharply with the dark shimmering window apertures. Like the subsequently constructed Water Place Tower, the One First National Bank of Chicago skyscraper is characterised by its austere design and use of contrasting materials.

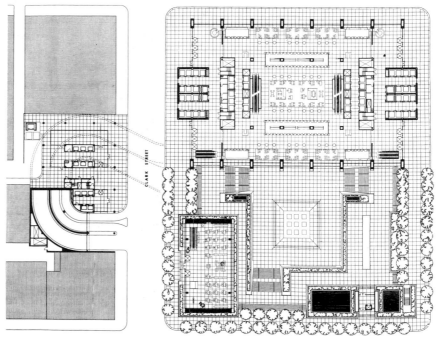

Ground floor

75

JOHN HANCOCK CENTER

Location	Chicago, IL, USA
Architect	Bruce Graham of SOM Skidmore, Owings & Merrill
Structural Engineer	Fazlur Khan of SOM
Completion	1969
Height	343 m (1 127 ft)
Volume	ca 1 100 000 m³
Use	Multiple use

Urban context

The design of the John Hancock Center, fondly nicknamed "Big John", was heavily influenced by the surroundings. The tower stands on Michigan Avenue in the vicinity of the Lake Shore Drive Apartments, located in one of the most attractive pedestrian and shopping areas in Chicago. The tower itself only occupies around fifty per cent of the plot. On the "Magnificent Mile" side of the tower, a sunken street courtyard connects the lower shop levels with the public areas. Towards the rear of the plot, a spiral car ramp leads to the parking levels.

When John Hancock commissioned this building, he insisted that the top floors be used for residential accommodation. Consequently architect Bruce Graham and engineer Fazlur Kahn had to develop a novel structure, using diagonal tubes, to permit mixed use of the interior and whilst retaining the scale and size of a 100-storey skyscraper.

The John Hancock Center is the largest multifunctional skyscraper in the world. The ground floors are given over to commercial use, with parking areas on the sixth to twelfth floors. Above this, there is office space extending up into the 41-storey. The upper storeys of the building are reserved for 711 apartments, complete with all the necessary infrastructure. At the very top of the tower, there is an observation deck, a restaurant and bar, which, at night offer an incredible view across the sea of lights in Chicago below. In principle, anyone living and working in the Hancock Center never need leave the building.

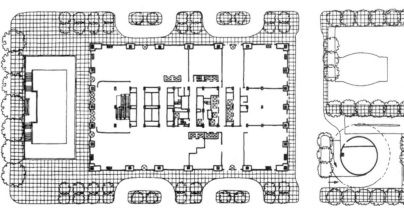

Ground floor

Structure

The floor area at the top of the tower is less than half the size of the ground floor space. The building's tapered form guarantees structural stability and efficient use of space. The outer piers and the horizontal spandrel beams form a steel tube, which is reinforced by diagonal bracing running through the floor slabs to create an extremely simple and structurally efficient system.

Circulation / Installations

The tower's centrally located core contains fifty lifts and five escalators, which transport up to 12 000 people a day. Express lifts directly link the entrance level with the transfer floors, the observation deck, and the restaurant at the very top of the tower.

Façade

The façade consists of five sections, each approximately 18-storeys high, defined by the exterior diagonal bracing tubes. In the top section, only half of the pattern is visible.

The external cladding is made of anodised aluminium with tinted bronze glass and bronze-coloured aluminium window frames. The two radio and television masts (both nearly 100 m high) on top of the tower form an integral element in the design of the building. At night, these illuminated masts are visible from afar, creating a landmark in Chicago's skyline.

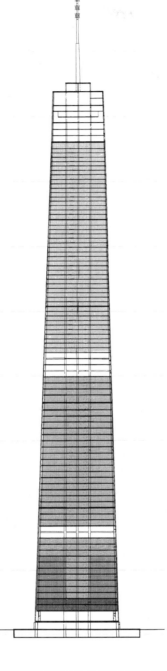

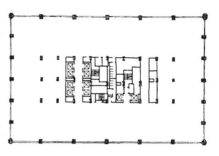

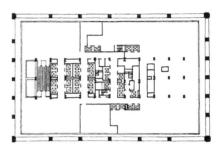

Apartment storey
Office storey
Shop storey

STANDARD BANK CENTRE

Location	Johannesburg, South Africa
Architect	Hentrich, Petschnigg & Partners
Completion	1970
Height	140 m (460 ft)
Volume	ca 145 000 m³
Use	Office, services

Urban context
The Standard Bank Centre stands opposite the Stock Exchange in Johannesburg's financial centre; there is a pedestrian link between the two buildings. To achieve maximum open space in the financial centre, the Standard Bank Centre was placed as far in the north-east corner of the site as possible. The plaza thus created is open to the public. In addition, there is a second, subterranean, pedestrian level connected to the main plaza via six escalators. The subterranean level contains a small shopping centre and a branch of the bank.

Structure
The Standard Bank tower is supported by a suspension system. The building consists of three separate units, arranged in vertical sequence. Each unit contains nine office floors, built around a load-bearing reinforced-concrete core. Between the office units there are structural floors with storey-high cantilevers to which eight hangers are fixed along the façade to support the floors. The horizontal loads are absorbed by the solid reinforced-concrete core.

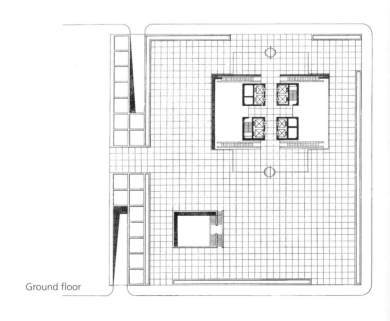

Ground floor

78

Circulation / Installations

The installations are located in the structural floors. The four towers at the very top are reserved for the technical rooms for the lift generators and motors, the cooling towers and the water tanks. The lifts and supply lines are housed in the core.

Façade

The façade design openly features the eight hangers, the structural floors, the horizontal concrete parapet elements and the 60-cm-wide plaster-finished balconies. Optimal interior illumination is provided by the continuous windows. The façade design is based on the interplay of horizontal and vertical elements.

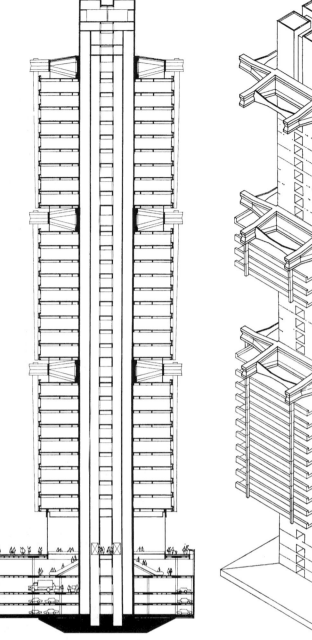

Structure diagram

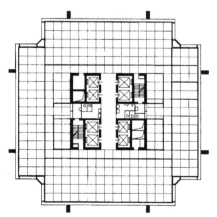

Typical storey

79

USX TOWER

Location	Pittsburgh, PA, USA
Architect	Harrison, Abramovitz & Abbe
Structural Engineer	Worthington, Skilling, Helle, Jackson
Completion	1970
Height	256 m (840 ft)
Volume	ca 1 000 000 m³
Use	Office, restaurant, exhibition

Urban context

The US Steel building (USX) is situated in Pittsburgh's "Golden Triangle" and was conceived to form the central point between the commercial centre and the "Civic Arena". Its triangular form and the two façades parallel to the river emphasise this concept. Rising to 256 metres, the building situated in the inner city is an important point of reference on Pittsburgh's skyline.

Structure

The exterior columns and the interior core, which is composed of slabs and columns, form the load-bearing structure. A horizontal frame in the loft links the core with the peripheral columns and serves to reinforce the structure. In addition, the columns on every third storey are linked to the core by means of the cantilevered floors, thus creating a system of primary storeys directly linked to the external load-bearing structure and the two secondary storeys above them. The secondary stories transfer their load via internal girders onto the primary storeys.

Circulation / Installations

The installations are located in four zones: in the basement, on the third and thirty-fourth storeys and in the two-storey loft (on the sixty-third and sixty-fourth floors). The triangular core contains three staircases and fifty-two lifts serving different floors. Owing to the triangular plan, the distance to the lifts and service areas is the same for all three open-plan office zones. The core accounts for approximately 30 per cent of the total volume of the building.

Façade

The exterior load-supporting structure and the skin are separate and mould the character of the façade. The steel columns stand out against the set-back curtain wall and accentuate the verticals, giving the façade a three-dimensional quality. The materialisation of the external load-bearing structure is quite striking: for the first time, the steel is exposed. This was made possible with a novel method – employed after performing fireproofing tests – of constructing the columns. The hollow steel columns, which are positioned approximately 90 cm in front of the façade, were filled with a water-based solution containing antifreeze and anticorrosion additives. Apart from its originality, this method saved the client about $1 million.

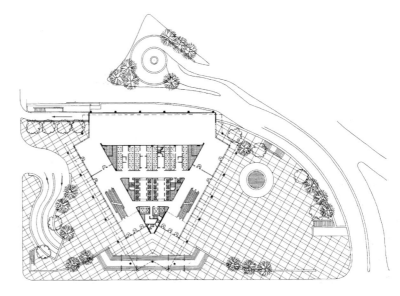

Site plan

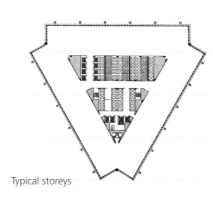
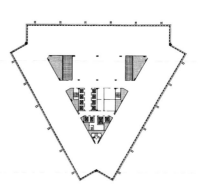

Typical storeys

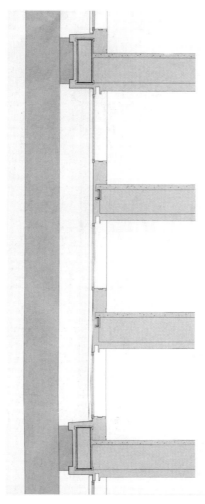
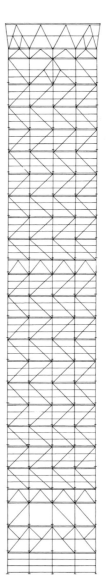

Façade detail
Structural grid

IBM BUILDING CHICAGO

Location	Chicago, IL, USA
Architect	L. Mies van der Rohe, C.F. Murphy & Ass.
Completion	1971
Height	230 m (755 ft)
Volume	ca 720 000 m³
Use	Office

Urban context

The IBM Building, situated parallel to State Street, is a 52-storey skyscraper with straight lineal contours. Its ground plan takes the shape of an extended rectangle. The building is set back on the site, thus creating a forecourt leading to the entrance and providing a view of the contrasting curves of the Marina City Towers. With 52-storeys, the IBM Building is one of the highest ever designed by Mies van der Rohe. The skyscraper has been positioned far enough to the north both to create a combined oblique perspective with the two neighbouring buildings, which are parallel to the river, whilst restricting the view from the residential blocks to the east as little as possible. Unfortunately, when the building was commissioned, the client decided against creating a connection to the river at street level.

Structure

The skyscraper has a steel skeleton structure with an inner central core. The supports have been built on a modular system analogous to that used in other skyscrapers designed by Mies van der Rohe.

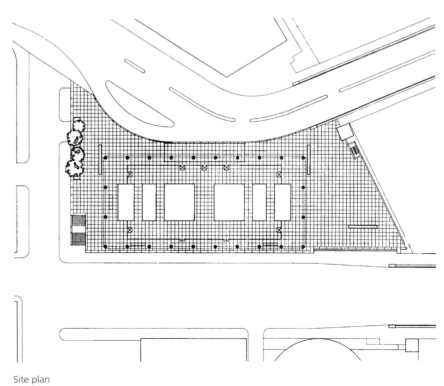

Site plan

Circulation / Installations

The building has highly sophisticated installations, including a complex integrated temperature control and heat recovery system. The technical rooms occupy two complete storeys, the sixteenth and the top floor, as can be seen from the façade.

Façade

The curtain wall of the IBM Building consists of a fully insulated external skin constructed after the following principle: insulating glazing 2.5 cm in thickness; a complete thermal separation between the inner and outer skin with a total thickness of only 5 cm; and a pressure equalisation system to fully seal the wall. The dark aluminium and the tinted bronze glass give the building the impression of precision and austerity of form. The double glazing functions as a thermal barrier between the outer and inner glass panel due to the pressure equalisation system, which equalises the pressure within the 5 cm thick "skin" and reduces air loss.

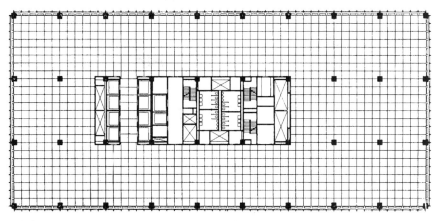

Typical storey

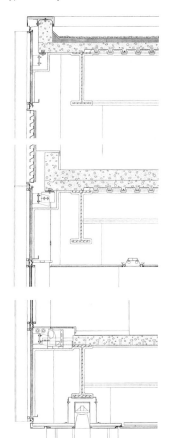

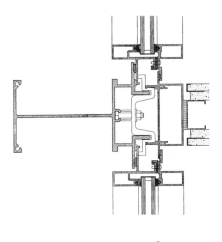

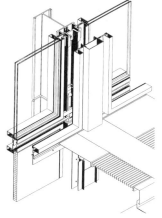

NAKAGIN CAPSULE TOWER

Location	Tokyo, Japan
Architect	Kisho Kurokawa
Completion	1972
Height	54 m (177 ft)
Volume	ca 6 000 m³, 132 residential capsules of 20 m³ each
Use	Residential

Urban context

The pressures caused by the expansion of Japan's major cities are giving rise to concepts for urban mega-structures (metabolism). The design for Capsule Tower envisages it as part of an endlessly extending mega-structure. Residential capsules are attached to vertical access towers linked to one another via footbridges. Conceived as mobile apartments, the capsules can, in theory, be detached at one point and remounted elsewhere.

Structure

The two reinforcing cores absorb the horizontal forces and transfer the vertical forces into the ground. In a future three-dimensional city, the footbridges holding the cores together could form part of a mega-frame. Capsules are attached to the core as independent static elements. In terms of manufacture, transportability and price, the concept of the residential capsules is modelled on the shipping container. The capsules consist of a welded metal frame enclosed in an insulating sheath.

Circulation / Installations

Each of the residential capsules constitutes an independent system with its own heating, ventilation and air conditioning. The capsule docks onto the service core, which contains the vertical shafts for the technical equipment. The core also contains stairs and a lift.

Façade

The façade is formed by the addition of the residential capsules, which are themselves already enclosed in a sheath. They are arranged according to an aesthetic principle based on the traditional wooden structure of Japanese temples.

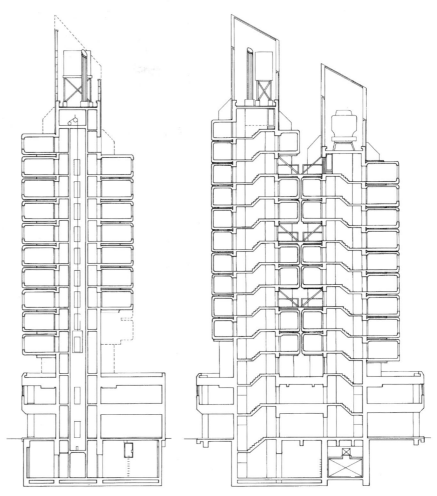

Cross section   Longitudinal section

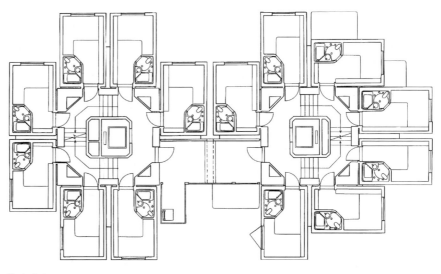

Typical storey

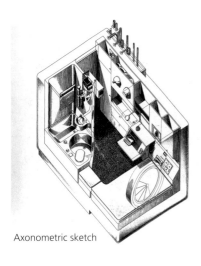

Axonometric sketch

TRANSAMERICA PYRAMID

Location	San Francisco, CA, USA
Architect	William L. Pereira & Associates
Structural Engineer	Chin and Hensolt
Completion	1972
Height	260 m (853 ft)
Volume	ca. 250 000 m³
Use	Services, office

Urban context

The Transamerica Pyramid, the headquarters of the Transamerica Corporation, is located between Montgomery Street and Columbus Avenue in San Francisco's financial district. In 1972, the project was unique in both height and in appearance.

The pyramid form was chosen for three reasons: it made it possible to circumvent the building regulations prescribing the ratio between a building's height and floor area; the tower was to serve as an advertisement for the Transamerica Corporation; finally, Pereira believed that a pyramid would let more light through to the streets. The Transamerica Pyramid was also one of the first skyscrapers to provide a formal alternative to the customary towers constructed in the International Style. Although there was active opposition to the building when construction started – the pyramid was attacked for being "insensitive, inappropriate, incongruous and in the wrong place" – it is now considered one of San Francisco's landmarks.

Structure

The building was secured against earthquakes in the following manner: Between the second and fifth storeys, twenty isosceles tetrahedrons were joined together. Their cones served as supports for the steel girders. A k-shaped structure situated between the second floor and the foundation was installed to provide further reinforcement. This creates a very rigid structure designed to ensure maximum safety and security.

Circulation / Installations

The installations are located in the 67-m-high apex of the pyramid, where the floor area is too small to permit reasonable office use.

The side "wings" of the pyramid contain the lift shafts, a fire-escape staircase and a chimney hood.

Façade

The façade is structured horizontally, with storey-high rows of windows. The facing is made of a special hardened cement paste. Additional reinforcement is also provided by the façade. On the twenty-seventh storey, there is a small observatory deck open to the public.

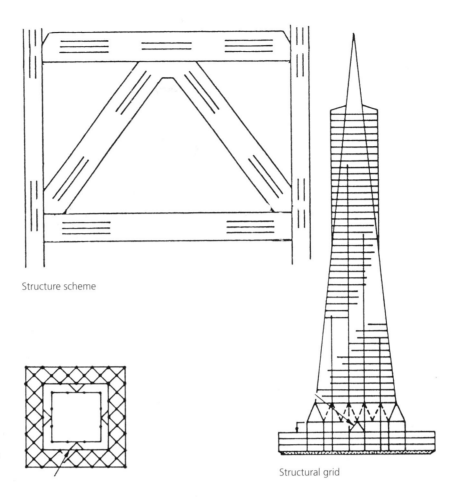

Structure scheme

Structural grid

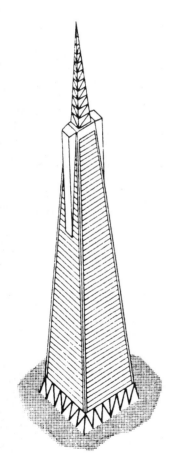

Axonometric view

WORLD TRADE CENTER

Location	New York, NY, USA
Architect	Minoru Yamasaki with Emery Roth & Sons
Structural Engineer	Skilling, Helle, Christiansen, Robertson
Completion	1972, 1973
Height	417 m (1,368 ft) I WTC 415 m (1,362 ft) II WTC
Volume	ca 5 000 000 m³
Use	Office

Urban context

The twin 110-storey towers of the World Trade Center dominate the Atlantic-side skyline of lower Manhattan and, according to the client, are intended to symbolise the importance of New York to world trade.

Approached from the Statue of Liberty, the side of the towers facing the waterfront creates an impressive gateway to New York.

Within the World Trade Center super block there is a large plaza, bordered on the Wall Street side by low buildings designed in dark tones, whilst the light Twin Towers mark the boundary towards the harbour. The plaza, raised one-storey above street level, is inaccessible to all motorised traffic. There is a large shopping arcade below the plaza, with restaurants and a connection to two of New York's major subway lines.

The earth excavated prior to the construction of the WTC was used as landfill on the Hudson River site for what later became Battery Park.

Structure

The columns in the façade form a densely-knit frame, which, together with the girder grid supporting the floors on each storey, create a steel tube structure which absorbs all the horizontal and vertical loads. The only columns within the building itself are located in the core area, thus enabling flexible allocation of usable floor space.

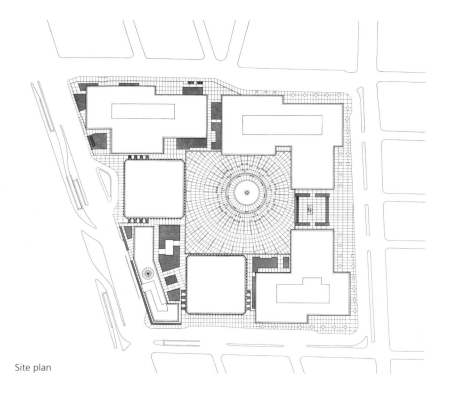

Site plan

Circulation / Installations

In order to minimise the area taken up by the core, the lift system has been divided into three vertical zones. This required the establishment of so-called sky lobbies on the forty-fourth and seventy-eighth storeys, which are accessed via twenty-three express lifts. Seventy-two local lifts operate from the sky lobbies. The passenger lift system is supplemented by four large goods lifts, which supply the restaurant at the top of the north tower and the viewing platform of the south tower.

Façade

The façade design is determined by the vertical load-bearing structure clad in stainless steel. In daylight, this lends the towers an almost monolithic character, obscuring the division into storeys and making it difficult to judge the scale of the buildings.

At ground-floor level, the façade opens to form a kind of plinth providing access to the plaza and the lower-lying street level. This doubling of the façade structure in the manner of the medieval Italian fortress towers avoids any sense of banality and, according to Huxtable, transforms the miniature module into a distinctive landmark.

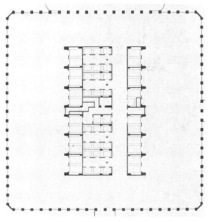

Typical storey

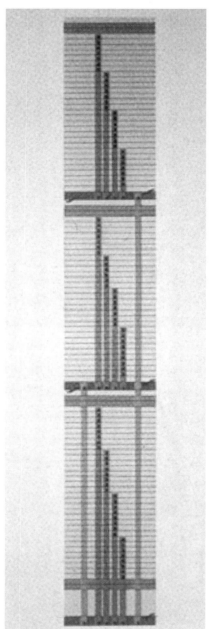

Circulation scheme

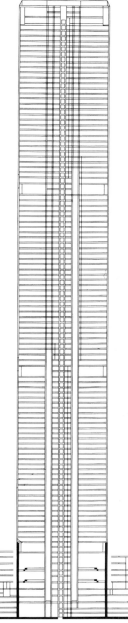

Section

FEDERAL CENTER

Location   Chicago, IL, USA

Architects   L. Mies van der Rohe in association
                with Schmidt, Garden & Erikson,
                C.F. Murphy Ass., A. Epstein & Sons

Completion   1973 (1959–73)

Height   Courthouse 120 m (395 ft)
                Office building 175 m (575 ft)
                Post pavilion 8 m (26 ft)

Volume   Courthouse ca 450 000 m³
                Office building ca 450 000 m³

Use   Court, administration,
                office, post office

Urban context

The three buildings making up the Federal Center occupy one-and-a-half blocks in the Loop, the central business district of Chicago. The post office and the office building share one of the blocks, which has two squares of different sizes – the smaller facing north-east and the larger, and consequently more important one, the south-west. The courthouse lies in the eastern part of Dearborn Street, which intersects the two blocks. The ground area of the buildings occupies less than half of the plot. Emphasis has been given to integrating the squares and entrance lobbies, which, being fully glazed, have been made part of the squares. In this convincing urban ensemble, with its carefully chosen volumetric proportions, Mies continued the general idea of the open inner-city square, as first realised in the United Nations complex and in the Lever House, both in New York, and further developed for his Seagram Building.

Structure

The two towers are steel skeleton structures with stiff nodal joints. There are additional, transverse, reinforced concrete walls in the elevator block. Both buildings have the same depth and details. The structural unit spacing is 8.52 m x 8.52 m. This grid is based, in turn, on a basic module of 1.42 m, so that six sections of moveable partition walls can be set between the supports. The standard storey height is 3.60 m.

Circulation / Installations

In both buildings, the access zones to the upper stories are located in the central cores, which lead uniformly through all stories. A special feature of the court building worth mentioning is that the court rooms have an independent circulation and lift system, which is more compact than that of the public areas, providing access to the offices of public prosecutors. Four of these special lifts also have direct access to the garage under the building so that prisoners can be taken directly to court rooms without their having to pass through public areas.

Façade

With the exception of the technical zones, all four façades of both towers are glazed uniformly with windows of equal size. The Federal Center is the last building in Chicago in which Mies used the principle of non-insulated outside walls. The columns are set back behind the façade, as is the case with curtain walls. The windows, which are linked to the double T-profiles, are spaced at equal intervals.

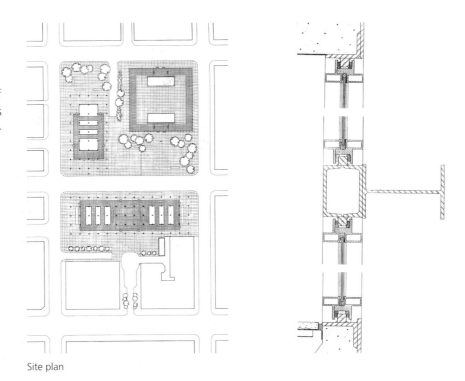

Site plan

Sections

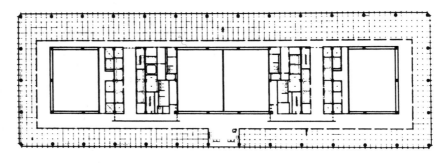

Court rooms storey

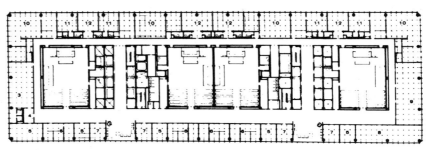

Office storey

SEARS TOWER

Location	Chicago, IL, USA
Architect	Bruce Graham of SOM Skidmore, Owings & Merrill
Structural Engineer	Fazlur R. Khan of SOM Skidmore, Owings & Merrill
Completion	1974
Height	443 m (1454 ft)
Volume	ca 1 700 000 m³
Use	Office, observation deck

Urban context

Until recently, the 100-storey-high Sears Tower was the world's tallest building. It was constructed to accommodate the 10 000 employees working for the department store giant Sears, Roebuck and Company and 6 000 tenants. The tower, with its innovative load-bearing structure, was developed under the direction of the brilliant civil engineer Fazlur Kahn. Soaring above the surrounding buildings in Chicago city centre, it is constantly present as a point of reference.

Structure

The building's height of 443 m was made possible by the development of a load-supporting structure consisting of a system of nine bundled tubes stacked on top of one another in box form. The horizontal edge-length of each of the bundles measures twenty-three metres. Not having any internal supports, the bundles are stabilised by the frame action of their compartments, which are formed by columns positioned at intervals of 4.60 m. The structure is further reinforced by two-storey-high braces positioned at the same height as the equipment rooms, i.e. at regular intervals of 100 m. This load-bearing system is particularly effective since – instead of relying on reinforcing cores – it activates the outside walls and all the other load-bearing structures in transferring the horizontal forces. Furthermore, the service cores – not having to fulfil a load-bearing function – could be planned freely to meet the requirements of both the circulation and the building installations. The number of tubes gradually diminishes towards the top, so that

only two are left at the crown of the tower. This set-back structure determines the mono-functional space-allocation programme accordingly: the open-plan offices are located on the lower floors; and as the floor area decreases towards the top of the building, the building's exclusivity and the sense of remoteness from the earth increase, too. The prime goal of the design was to accentuate the immense height of the building as well as its superior structure. Because the tube modules are set back, the silhouette of the tower varies according to one's point of view.

Circulation / Installations

Four huge ventilation systems are housed in floors 106 to 109. The building's express lifts ascend from the ground floor to the skydeck in less than one minute. Some fifty local lifts link the individual floors and parts of the building via transfer floors.

Façade

In combination with the modest load-bearing structure, the glass-and-metal façade lends the building the appearance of a shining abstract sculpture – designed to be viewed from afar – which seems to rise unexpectedly out of the ground. One has the feeling that it could be built even higher.

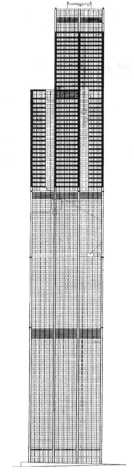

Elevation

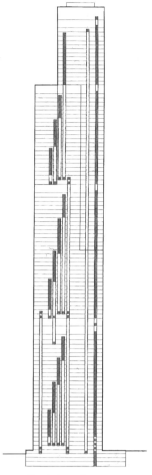

Circulation scheme

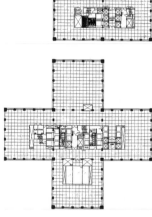

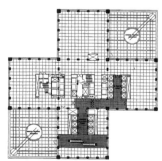

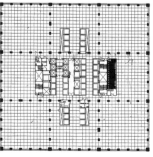

Typical storey

OVERSEAS CHINESE BANK

Location	Singapore
Architect	I.M. Pei & Partners
Structural Engineer	Ove Arup & Partners
Completion	1980
Height	ca 200 m (660 ft)
Volume	ca 300 000 m³
Use	Services, office

Urban context

Over the past ten years, the shortage of land has induced Singapore to increasingly develop upwards on the basis of an overall-planning strategy. In the city centre, small colonial-style office buildings constructed under Chinese influence have given way to skyscrapers. When the Overseas Chinese Bank was completed in 1980, its fifty-one storeys made it the highest building in Singapore. It was erected in the historical Chinese trading centre where it replaced the old company headquarters. The building made no attempt to adapt to its surroundings, demonstrating instead that it was part of a future skyscraper skyline in the megapolis of Singapore.

Structure

In order to create a clear-span bank hall, a system was chosen that would transfer the load of the fourteen office floors above the hall via a transfer storey on the fourth floor, and then into the ground through four solid concrete columns. On the nineteenth and thirty-fifth floors, transfer storeys carry the loads into the semicircular core at the side. This load-bearing system permitted the construction of a clear-span conference floor and a penthouse on the roof.

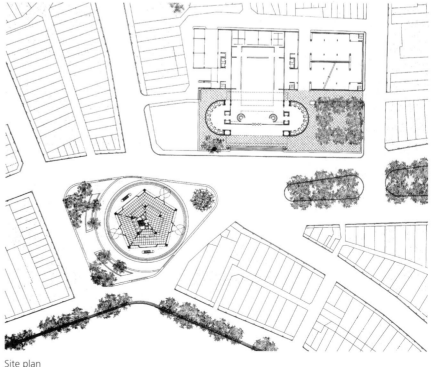

Site plan

Circulation / Installations

To attain maximum flexibility in the arrangement of the office floors, all of the service units, comprising nine lifts each together with wet rooms, are situated in the two semicircular concrete cores at the side. The supply shafts for the equipment rooms, which are located on the roof and in the transfer storeys, are also located in the core areas.

Façade

"As solid as a rock" was the bank's motto. The load-bearing system manifests itself in the external appearance of the building. Both the concrete cores at the sides and the transfer storeys are clad in white Sardinian granite slabs, creating a smooth surface. This provides a striking contrast to the three cantilevered office-floor units. To avoid excessive heating in Singapore's tropical climate, the windows were set back slightly from the façade, giving this part of the skin a rough surface texture.

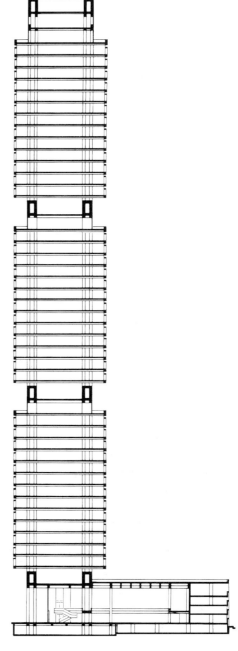

Cross section

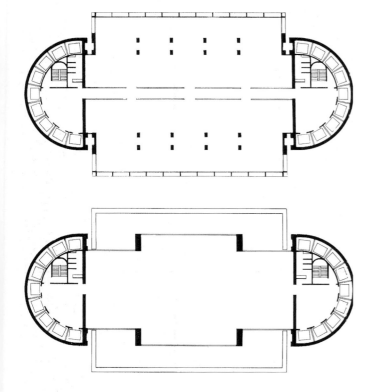

UNITED NATIONS
PLAZA I AND II

Location	New York, NY, USA
Architect	Kevin Roche, John Dinkeloo & Associates
Structural Engineer	I: Weiskopf & Pickworth II: The Office of Irwin Cantor
Completion	I: 1975 II: 1983
Height	150 m (492 ft)
Volume	230 000 m³
Use	Hotel, office

Urban context

The towers of UN Plaza I and II located not far from downtown Manhattan. The two equally tall blocks are linked by a common plinth and two bridges. Although the main axis of the city connects the skyscraper zones of downtown and midtown Manhattan, the mirror-glass towers have been consciously placed at right angles to this axis, and directly face the UN Headquarters and East River. With their tapered contours and set-backs, the towers respond to the surrounding developments. Their sculptural form was also determined by the Zoning Laws, which stipulated a maximum width of 20 m for the hotel located at the top.

Structure

The vertical loads of the two 39-storey skyscrapers are transferred directly into the ground through the clad steel columns. Owing to its stiffness, the steel multi-frame structure, customary in New York, absorbs horizontal and torsional loads.

Circulation / Installations

Vertical access is provided via a core zone containing two staircases and various lift systems (the hotel and the offices have their own lifts). In the middle zone, access has been arranged so as to shorten the escape routes. Vertical media distribution takes place through a number of shafts, whilst the hollow ceilings permit horizontal distribution. The swimming pool, which provides water for fire fighting, also requires an additional dehumidification system for the enclosing space. There is an alarm system and a special smoke-extraction shaft to ensure safety in case of fire. Owing to thermal considerations, the glass façade is composed of green-blue-tinted mirror-glass. A mobile cradle is located on the roof for cleaning the windows.

Façade

Although the UN Plaza I/II buildings were constructed in succession, the very same design principles were followed with respect to realisation, interior finishing and façade design, thus giving the two buildings a uniform character. They owe their abstract appearance to the regular quadratic grid, whilst set-backs accentuate the impact of the reflections. The curtain-wall glazing seems to be draped over the steel skeleton, and opens at the bottom to form a continuous canopy round the entire structure. The mirror-glass façade allows independent and diversified design of the interior rooms. Even so, the façade symbolically refers to the interior, which where an elegant atmosphere, however cool and artificial, prevails. A striking feature of the architecture is that attention has been paid to the tiniest details.

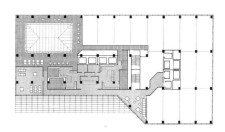

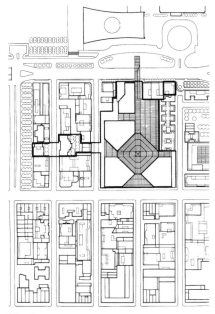

Site plan

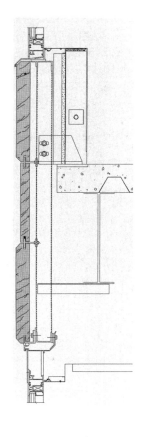

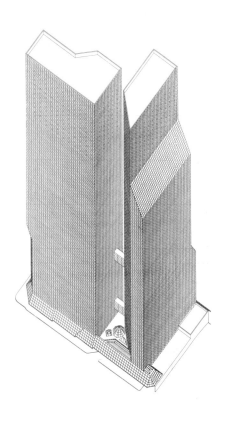

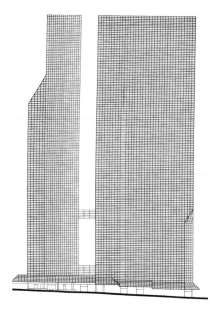

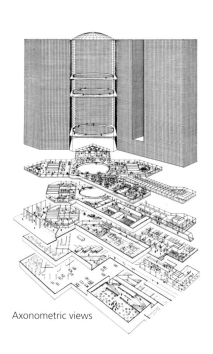

Axonometric views

97

JOHN HANCOCK TOWER

Location	Boston, MA, USA
Architect	Henry Cobb of Pei Cobb Freed & Partners
Structural Engineer	The Office of J. Ruderman
Completion	1976
Height	240 m (788 ft)
Volume	ca 630 000 m³
Use	Office (life insurance corporation)

Urban context

The John Hancock Tower rises directly behind the historical brick buildings lining the riverbank in Old Boston. Various measures were taken to soften the impact at this historic site of the building's enormous height and massiveness: firstly, the narrower, less-obstructing side of the tower was constructed to face Copley Square in central Boston. Secondly, the idea of dematerialising the building was implemented using, for the first time, a mirror-glass façade. An ominous monolithic effect was thus avoided and the building itself transformed into a background and setting, especially for Trinity Church, which is reflected in the skyscraper's façade.

Structure

The John Hancock Tower is a 60-storey building with a conventional steel-skeleton structure and curtain-wall glass façade. Its elongated form is based on an extruded parallelogram. After several glass panes had loosened and crashed to the ground, doubts were expressed about the building's ability to withstand wind forces. To deal with this danger, an additional 1 650 tonnes were used to reinforce the structure. It was found that the movement caused by wind pressure on the sail-like building can have an adverse affect on users' well-being.

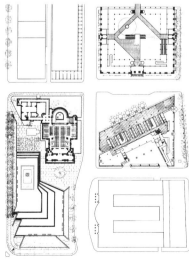

Site plan

98

Circulation / Installations

The supply shafts and vertical-access cores are arranged along the tower's main axis, thus permitting greater flexibility in ground plan division. "Tuned mass dampers" were later installed in the top storey to achieve an effective reduction in translation and torsion, thereby improving the quality of life inside the building.

Façade

The façade comprises 10 334 identically shaped mirror-glass panes. The building is fully glazed with storey-high fenestration, thus establishing a legible scale whilst simultaneously creating a highly abstract homogeneous surface.

Axonometric detail

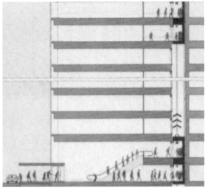

Section of lower floors

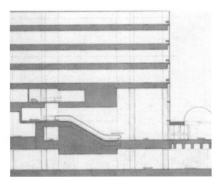

Section of lower floors

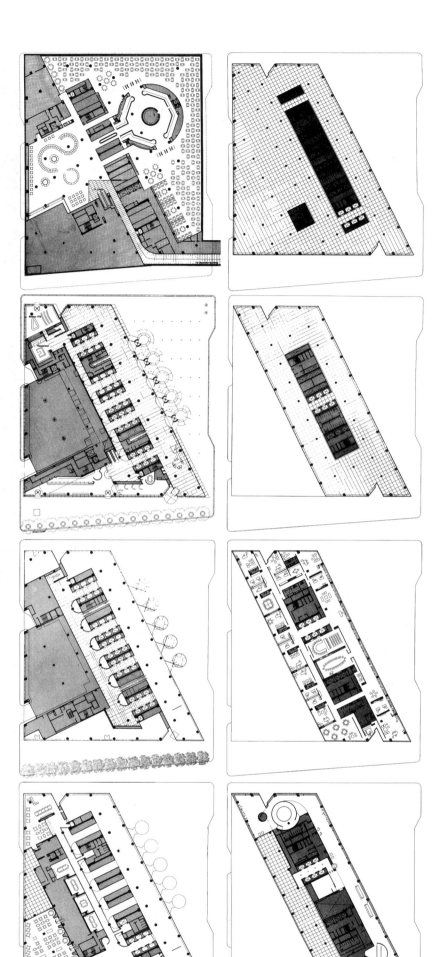

99

WESTIN PEACHTREE PLAZA HOTEL

Location: Atlanta, GA, USA

Architect: John Portman & Associates

Structural   John Portman & Associates
Engineer

Completion   1976

Height: 221 m (725 ft)

Volume: ca 200 000 m³

Use: Congress center and hotel

Urban context

This crystalline urban context, which dominates all else, marks the commercial centre of Atlanta. The introverted plinth, out of which the Peachtree Plaza Hotel rises, establishes a clear boundary between the building and its surroundings. There is now a new connecting level in the upper section of the plinth, where shopping malls create links with the lower levels. The Peachtree Plaza Hotel stands for a hotel conception that aims to create an urban microcosm within the hotel itself; it contains conference rooms, bars, shops, a variety of restaurants and large public atriums – a celebration of hotel life for the guests.

Structure

The Peachtree Plaza Hotel is a reinforced concrete structure. Its plinth area consists of a support-grid, whilst the concrete façade provides part of the reinforcement. The fully glazed hotel tower is stabilised by a cylindrical reinforced concrete core. Inside the tower, the load of the interior walls are transferred under a concrete collar visible from outside the building via a cantilever system – beneath a concrete collar visible from the outside – into the massive, round concrete columns inside the atrium.

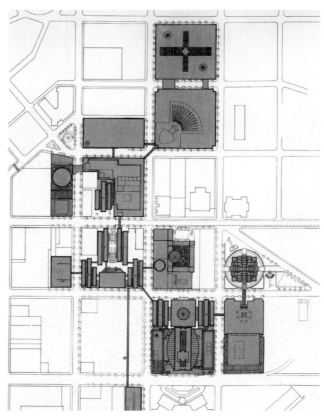

Site plan

Circulation / Installations

Apart from fulfilling a load-bearing function, the concrete core also houses the vertical access system. Ten passenger and two service lifts, as well as staircases and media ducts, link all the storeys. There is an impressive panorama lift to take passengers straight to the rotating restaurant on the roof. A similar lift provides a direct link between the two lower floors containing the conference rooms. Access to the first five storeys is provided by stairs located at the sides of the plinth, which are shown to their full advantage in the atrium.

Façade

The fully glazed tower of the Peachtree Hotel provides a marked contrast to the concrete façade. The exterior of the hotel is impressive, especially when viewed from afar. Owing to its reflecting façade, the tower dominates the Atlanta skyline. The façade of the three restaurant storeys distinguishes itself from the upper equipment floor and the lower hotel rooms by its non-reflecting surface elements.

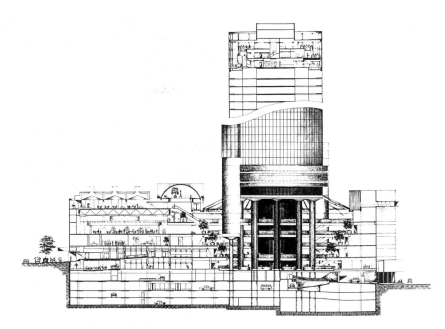

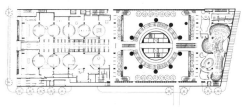

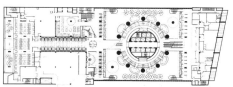

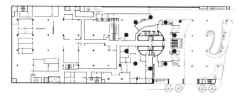

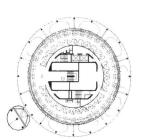

Plinth storeys

Tower storeys

WATER TOWER PLACE

Location	Chicago, IL, USA
Architect	Loebl, Schlossmann, Bennett, Dart & Hackl with C.F. Murphy Associates
Structural Engineer	C.F. Murphy Associates
Completion	1976
Height	262 m (859 ft)
Volume	ca 1 100 000 m³
Use	Multiple

Urban context

Situated directly next to the John Hancock center, the Water Tower Place building derives its name from the adjacent Water Tower and Pumping Station. This famous landmark, built in 1869 in imitation Gothic style, was one of the few buildings in Chicago to survive the Great Fire of 1871.

Seventy-four storeys high, Water Tower Place comprises two different sections, a horizontal podium and a tower, and its constituent elements make it into a miniature city within a city block. With restaurants, cinemas, two department stores and over 100 smaller shops in the 7-storey base, it is one of the world's most multi-functional buildings. The tower itself contains offices, the Ritz-Carlton Hotel with 400 rooms on 15 floors, and 260 apartments on a further 40 floors.

The plinth, with its shopping mall grouped around an atrium, stands directly on the "Magnificent Mile" on Michigan Avenue. Situated in front of the two entrances to the department stores is a two-storey arcade. At the rear of the site, on an internal access road, are the entrances to the various sections of the tower, which is located to the side in the rear corner – as far from the John Hancock Center as possible – so as not to obstruct the view of and from "Big John".

Structure

Water Tower Place was the tallest reinforced concrete building of its time. The use of high-strength ferroconcrete made it possible to build the number of storeys originally planned.

Circulation / Installations

Vertical access is provided by three distinct systems; express lifts, local lifts and escalators, which combine to transport up to 18 000 people every hour into each of the public and private areas.

Façade

In contrast to the Hancock Center, the various uses of the building are expressed in its composition and façades. The plinth, which has no apertures except at street level, is a clear expression of the commercial use of its interior, while the narrow tower accommodates the apartments and hotel. The white-veined marble cladding of the austere, rectangular grid structure and the apparent blackness of the glass in the window spaces create a stark contrast to the uniform treatment of the diagonally striped, monotone neighbouring building. In its urban context, these features assign the building a shrewdly considered role in relation to all the better-known buildings in its immediate and wider surroundings.

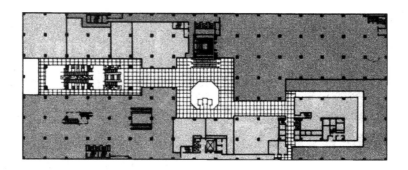
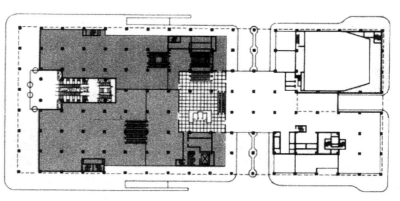
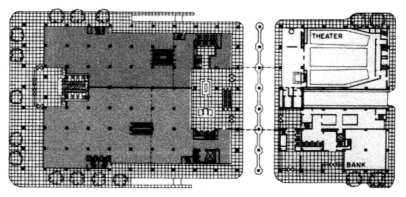

3rd floor / 1st floor / Ground floor

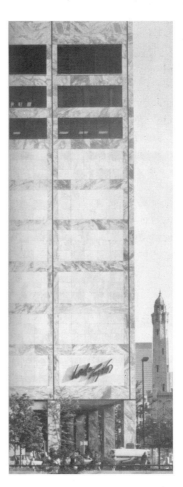

CITICORP CENTER

Location	New York, NY, USA
Architect	Hugh Stubbins & Associates with Emery Roth & Sons
Structural Engineer	LeMessurier Associates and the Office of James Ruderman
Completion	1977
Height	279 m (915 ft)
Volume	ca 650 000 m³
Use	Multiple

Urban context

From its inception, the Citicorp Bank building presented a challenge to the the urban disposition. The site was free for development except for the corner, where St. Peter's Lutheran Church stood. The church reached an agreement whereby it sold its air rights to Citicorp and received, in return, a new church on the same site, separate from the Citicorp building and with open sky above it. These requirements led to a unique engineering solution – the supports carrying the 55-storey office block were positioned in the middle of the façade. This allowed the church to be a free-standing structure and permitted the creation of an open public plaza at street level, receiving plenty of daylight.

This striking structural solution gives further emphasis to the strategic location of the Citicorp Center. Moreover, the forty-five degree angle of the Citicorp Center roof makes it instantly recognisable from a distance on the Manhattan skyline. At the same time, a very urbane public space has been created in an attempt to establish direct contact to people via the plaza, church and subway in the central base support.

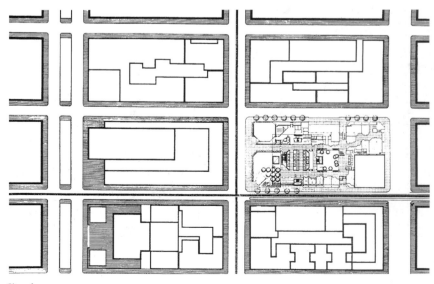

Site plan

Structure

Together with the central core, the four 114-feet-high, load-bearing supports carry the entire weight of the skyscraper. The tower is divided into six units of eight floors each, defined by diagonal, V-shaped steel buttressing. Within each system of forces, the vertical forces are transferred from the corners into the middle of the sides, where they are then further transferred into the foundations via the four supports. This skyscraper was one of the first tall buildings to be fitted with a tuned-mass-damper (TMD), a 400-ton, computer-controlled concrete block situated on the top of the building and used to equalise the effects of wind sway movements.

Circulation / Installations

The central core, located in the center of the tower, also houses a total of twenty-two lifts, which, for the most part, have double-floor cabins to transport passengers from two floors simultaneously, thus saving both space and time. The emergency staircases are also located within the centre core as well as in three of the four façade supports.

Façade

The façade consists of alternate bands of clear, reflecting glass and shiny aluminium panels. This smooth, gleaming external skin is intended to underline the distinct external appearance of the tower and make it stand out against the surrounding buildings.

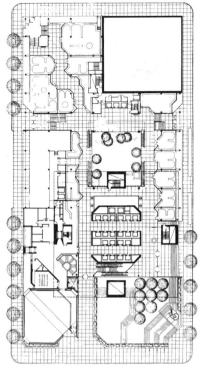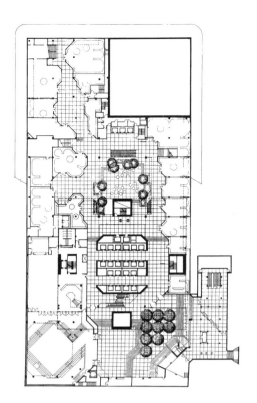

Ground floor

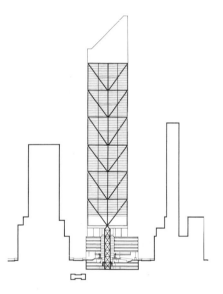

Structural grid

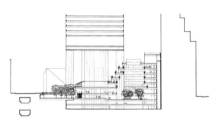

Plinth section

RENAISSANCE CENTER

Location	Detroit, MI, USA
Architect	John Portman & Associates
Structural Engineer	John Portman & Associates
Completion	1977
Height	221 m (725 ft)
Volume	ca 1 800 000 m³ (the entire complex)
Use	Detroit Plaza Hotel, offices, apartments, shopping centre

Urban context

By developing novel urban structures, a number of investors sought to stem increasing migration from the centre of Detroit to the suburbs. The name Renaissance Center reflects their ambition to revive the city centre. Roads border the site on three sides, with the river forming a natural barrier on the fourth. An earlier design envisaged linking the complex and the city via a footbridge crossing the river. The complex is an organic type of structure. Two gigantic plinths unite the 73-storey Renaissance One Hotel towers and the six lower office towers on a common base. The buildings were designed to provide views in all directions. The complex stands like an island in its urban environment.

Structure

The hotel tower is based on a typical Portman statics concept: a tubular concrete core containing the circulation and the installation shafts both transfers the greater part of the vertical forces downwards and provides horizontal reinforcement. The outer side of the core is supplemented by an external ring of columns. There is a table-like support at the transition from the plinth to the tower. Every second column in the ring is continued down through the plinth to function as a solid support.

Circulation / Installations

The core forms the backbone of the tower. The horizontal distribution is located in the floors of the individual storeys. Mechanical and electrical installations are integrated into the peripheral noise-protection walls. There are sixteen lifts and a number of staircases in the hotel tower. Only half of the lifts ascend through the upper section. The external panorama lifts are a special feature of the complex.

Façade

The most distinguishing characteristic of this Portman project is the diversified design of the interior space, i.e. of the atrium and the hotel. The plinth, with its solid concrete façade, creates a clear demarcation between the complex and the surrounding area. The towers have reflecting mirror glass façades with a variety of grid patterns.

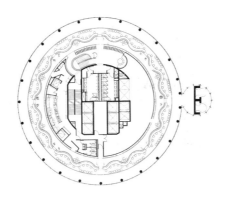

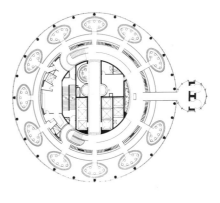

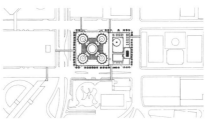

Site plan

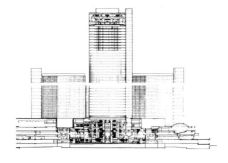

BANCO DE BILBAO

Location	Madrid, Spain
Architect	F.J. Saenz de Oiza
Structural Engineer	F. Casado y J. Manterda
Completion	1979
Height	102 m (334 ft)
Volume	ca 70 000 m³
Use	Bank, office

Urban context

This monolithic building functions as a striking point of reference in Madrid. From a distance, one can only identify the horizontal stratification. As the façades display no other articulation, the tower seems to any attempt to gauge its dimensions. The corner plot is accentuated by the rectangular ground plan. At basement level, the building is crossed diagonally by the underground. The architecture of the new structure supplies simple and direct answers on how to deal with the problems posed by accommodating a complex structural organisation in a vertical building.

Structure

The load-bearing structure of the building comprises two reinforced cores, each 125 m high. The cantilever structure divides the building into six load-bearing units in the form of conventional steel supports. This type of structure allowed the construction of a suspended ground floor, which makes the building appear to float in the air.

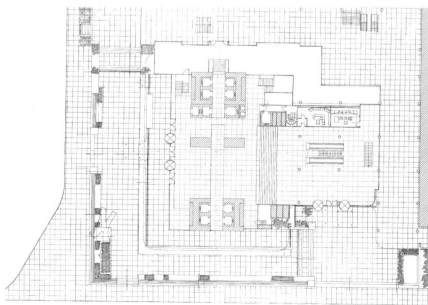

Ground floor

Circulation / Installations

All the vertical connections, such as the lifts and technical installations, are housed in the two solid cores. The stairwell and an additional shaft for technical installations are located at the center of the building. The 10th, 20th and 30th floors are reserved for the technical installations, which are supplemented by the main technical room in the basement.

Façade

The façade composition realises the idea of a unified plate-glass surface. Stratification is achieved by using horizontal bands, which create shadow and serve as walkways for cleaning and maintaining the façade. Matt green curtain walls on the west façade create additional shadow from the 10th floor upwards. The window structure is made of "Cor-Ten" steel and double-glazing using "Dialux" thermoglass.

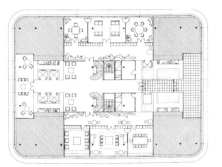
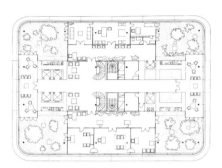
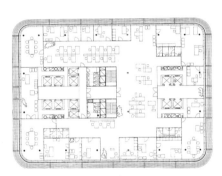
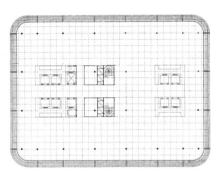

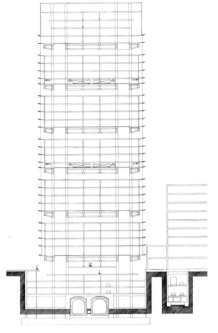

Longitudinal section

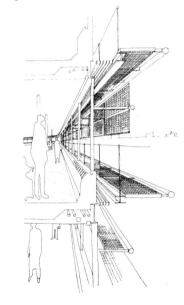

Perspective view of façade

M.L.C. CENTRE

Location	Sydney, Australia
Architect	Harry Seidler
Structural Engineer	Civil & Civic, Lehman & Talty, DT Broughton & Ass.
Structural Consultant	Pier Luigi Nervi
Completion	1978
Height	244 m (800 ft)
Volume	ca 400 000 m³
Use	Shops, office

Urban context

This white, polygonal tower was constructed on a site raised above the adjacent streets. The plan forms a square with trimmed corners; the short edges run parallel to the streets bordering the building. In this way, the 65-storey building respects the course of the underground railway tunnels. Access to the M.L.C. Centre is via two squares leading up to the tower from street level. The Centre is part of a complex which includes restaurants, shops, cinemas, open plazas and the Royal Theatre, and features works by contemporary artists such as Josef Albers and Alexander Calder. The radial floor arrangement further emphasizes the position of the building. The architectural idiom expressed by the M.L.C. Centre also characterizes the other tower by Seidler, located on Sydney's Australia Square. In addition, both structures greatly recall the programme for an ideal church formulated by Alberti during the Renaissance.

Structure

In technical terms, the M.L.C. Centre is a tube-in-tube concrete construction. The vertical load is borne by the central core, which contains the building's technical installations, and the eight columns at the corners. The required rigidity is achieved through the special form of the vertical supports. Façade and core are connected by ribbed ceilings. The most interesting of these is to be found in the lobby, where the ceiling required special reinforcement and reflects the flow of structural forces. It bears the unmistakable stamp of P.L. Nervi.

Circulation / Installations

The building has twenty-four lifts ascending from the ground floor. Like the other technical installations, they are contained in the core of the tower.

Façade

The façade is faced with white quartz and articulates the clear, rationalistic language that typifies this building. During construction, horizontal, pre-fabricated concrete sections were fixed between the vertical corner columns and then filled with cement. These 11- to 19-m beams have a double-T-girder cross section, which makes them extremely resistant to bending. The windows are recessed, so that the horizontal structural elements also provide protection from the sun.

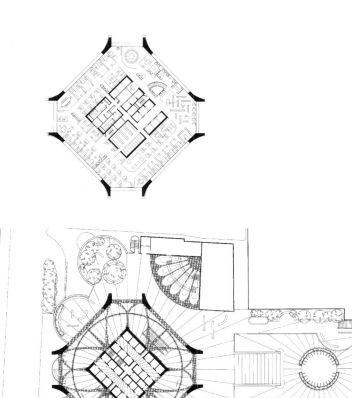

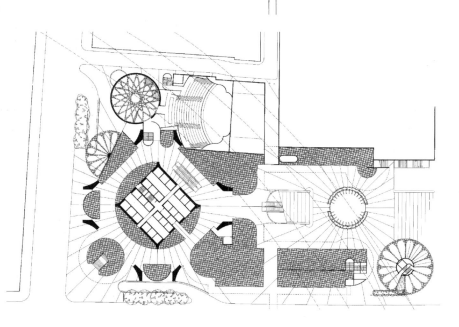

XEROX CENTER

Location	Chicago, IL, USA
Architect	Murphy / Jahn & Associates
Structural Engineer	Cohen, Barretto, Marchertas, Inc.
Completion	1980
Height	120 m (393 ft)
Volume	ca 280 000 m³
Use	Bank, office

Urban context

An additional corner building that complemented the site was designed for the corner of Dearborn Street and Monroe Street in the middle of the Loop, which is served by three curving overhead railway lines. Murphy and Jahn wanted to take a clear stand at this important location in the inner city. The building has the form of a rounded corner. The ground floor is accessed diagonally, whilst the façades, thanks to the curved edge, look as if they were made of one single piece of material.

One of the rear sides is linked to the lower neighbouring building containing parking spaces.

Like the existing buildings, the Xerox Center stands on the edge of the plot on the Monroe Street side. On the Dearborn Street side, however, it is set back 7 m.

Structure

The building is a reinforced concrete structure with a 6 m x 6 m column grid. In the middle of the building, there is a reinforcing core containing the vertical access links. This permits spacious open-plan offices that can be arranged to suit individual requirements, thus meeting the speculative intentions of the project investors.

Circulation / Installations

The building is supplied by two double-storey equipment floors. One of these is located above the bank and serves just over half of the tower. The other is located at the very top and in the P-shaped penthouse.

Vertical access is provided via two lift zones with eight lifts each. Here, too, one of the zones covers a little more than half the height of the building. Escalators are installed in the bank storeys.

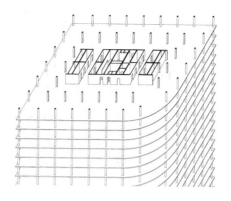

Façade

A thin skin of aluminium and glass stretches over the structure, with the proportion of glass ranging from 50–75 per cent. On the one hand, this reduces solar heating whilst, on the other hand, the horizontal bands and storey-high fenestration accentuate the curved form.

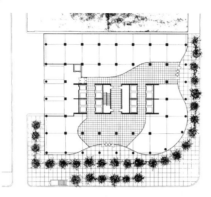

Ground floor

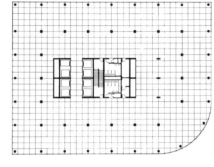

Typical storey

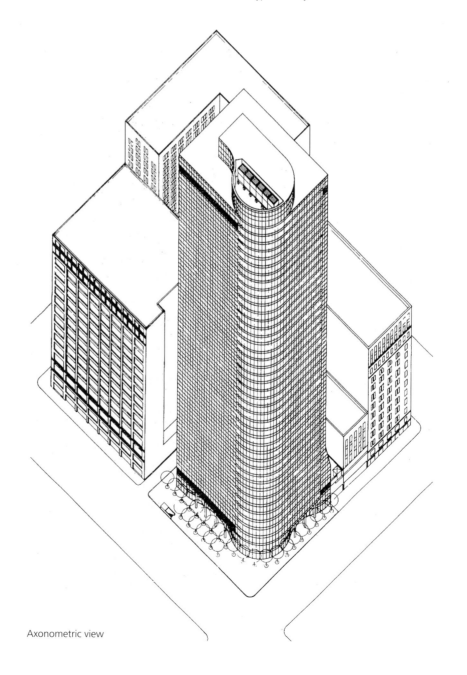

Axonometric view

IBM BUILDING NEW YORK

Location	New York, NY, USA
Architect	Edward Larrabee Barnes
Structural Engineer	The Office of James Ruderman with LeMessurier Associates
Completion	1983
Height	ca 170 m (560 ft)
Volume	ca 360 000 m³
Use	Office

Urban context

The 43-storey IBM Building is situated at the corner of Madison Avenue and 57th Street. On the east side of the plot stands the Trump Tower by Der Scutt and, on the south side, the AT&T Building by Philip Johnson. The three buildings form a densely built complex of postmodernist structures creating a covered area – extending from 55th to 57th Street – between 5th Avenue and Madison Avenue. Designed in the shape of a prisma cut away on five sides, the IBM Building provides different views relative to the standpoint of the observer.

The north-eastern corner of this self-supporting structure is cut away at street level to create more room for pedestrians.

On the south-western corner, the building is supplemented by a large atrium, the Garden Piazza, which is planted with bamboo. Between the IBM Building and the Trump Tower, there is a covered area, which simultaneously serves as a link to 56th and 57th Street. The atrium and the street virtually pass into one another.

Structure

The building is a steel skeleton structure based on a rather irregularly arranged column grid. In the middle of the prisma, lifts have been installed between the columns. Together with the fire-escape staircases, the lift shafts help reinforce the structure. The atrium has a steel structure.

Circulation / Installations

The IBM Building contains two self-supporting lift-cores. Two additional blocks house lifts as well as other equipment and sanitation shafts. Not all of the eighteen lifts ascend to the office floors; some only travel to the sixth floor.

The atrium is partly supplied by natural ventilation. Part of the building equipment and installations are housed in the top two storeys; 30% of the ground floor area and approximately 20% of the office-floor area are reserved for technical installations.

Façade

The building is clad with dark-green polished granite and green glass, thus creating an elegant, uniform impression. The Garden Plaza is glazed like a winter garden making it light and creating a welcoming atmosphere.

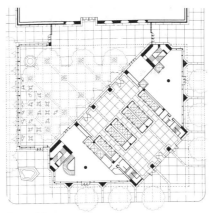

Ground floor

Restaurant storey

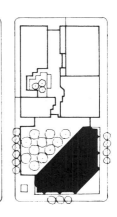

Site plan

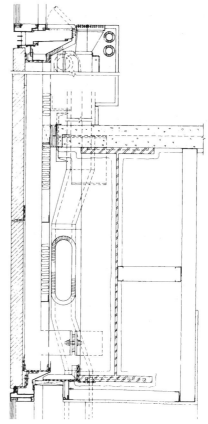

NATIONAL COMMERCIAL BANK

Location   Jeddah, Saudi Arabia

Architect   SOM Skidmore Owings & Merrill

Structural   SOM
Engineers

Completion   1983

Height   126 m (413 ft)

Volume   220 000 m^3

Use   Bank, office

Urban context

Although Saudi Arabia has traditionally been a country of low buildings, the shape of the site and the magnificent view of the Red Sea inspired the decision to build a high-rise structure of twenty-seven storeys. Adjacent to the triangular tower is a circular garage with 400 parking spaces. The plot has an area of approximately 11,800 m^3 and is located between the old town and the sea. In accordance with local building traditions, the structure is turned inwards to shield users from heat and sunlight. All the office areas face the internal triangular courtyards, which have been cut out of the body of the structure. Two of the courtyards are seven storeys high and face the town, while the third, positioned in the middle of the building, is nine storeys high and faces the sea. The integration of these courtyards into the ground plan has created two relatively narrow V-shaped converging wings with floor areas of approximately 1 700 m^3.

Structure

The building is constructed of reinforced concrete and stiffened at the triangular corners and the service core on the north-east side of the tower. Due to the eccentric double core, the possibilities for subdividing the office floors are almost unlimited. Furthermore, thanks to this design, the banking hall, which is located on the ground floor and occupies the entire ground-plan area of the triangle, has been kept free of any built-in units.

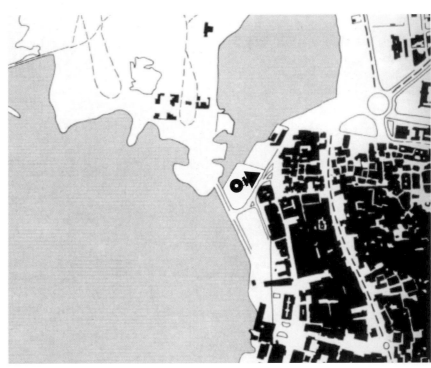

Site plan

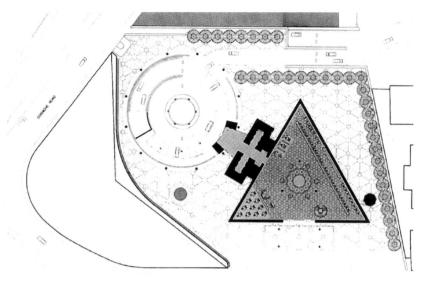
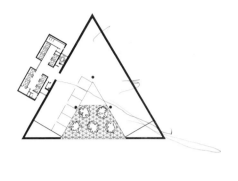

Site plan / Typical storey

Circulation / Installations

All of the open-plan offices face away from the sun and towards the inner courtyards. The three courtyards overlap in the centre of the structure, creating a light and ventilation shaft ascending the entire height of the building and directing heat from the courtyards upwards through natural circulation. All lifts, stairwells and sanitary units, together with the installation shafts, are located in a double core on the north-east side of the triangular tower, whose wall is not interrupted by the inner courtyards.

Façade

The travertine surfacing is extremely modest in appearance. On closer viewing, the different storeys can be detected in the arrangement of the façade slabs. Apart from this, every effort has been made not to spoil the prismatic form of the tower. Even with the massive clefts formed by the inner courtyards, the basic form of the structure has been maintained. The large openings on two sides of the building reveal the more fragile glass surfaces on the inner façades.

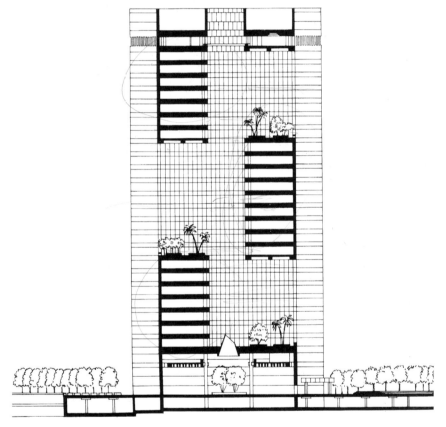

Cross section

117

TORHAUS GLEISDREIECK

Location   Frankfurt, Germany

Architect   O.M. Ungers

Completion   1983

Height   115 m (377 ft)

Volume   ca 200 000 m³

Use   Service facilities for the Frankfurt
                Fair; offices, conference rooms

Urban context

The Torhaus Gleisdreieck fulfils various
urban functions:
– the establishment of a vertical link
  between the two parts of the exhibition site over the railway property
– helping to transform the Frankfurt
  Fair into a huge gateway to the city
– creating service facilities, offices and
  conference rooms
Ungers made use of three elements: a
plinth, a stone structure and a glass
building. The plinth fills the entire plot
and contains the general service functions for the Fair operations. There is a
promenade platform at the top.
The tower consists of two interlinked
structures: a stone building and a glass
building. The latter houses the conference rooms. All three elements are
united in the lower section of the glass
building, as the 9-storey "public area"
reveals.

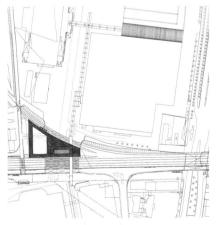

Site plan

118

Structure

The glass tower, the brick building and the plinth are solid structures clad in brick and glass, with the two cores serving as reinforcement.

Circulation / Installations

The shafts, emergency staircases and lift installations are located in the two cores.

Although the heating station in the south-eastern corner of the plinth is set off from the rest of the structure by means of a joined section, it is nevertheless integrated optically into the whole.

Façade

On one side of the building, the plinth and the tower form a single flush wall, creating, in the middle section, an oversized window that reappears in the strict grid design of the window apertures.

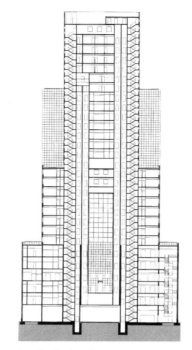 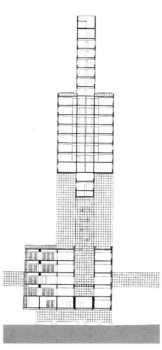

Longitudinal section   Cross section

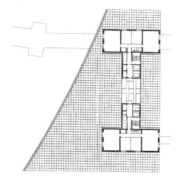 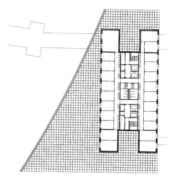

 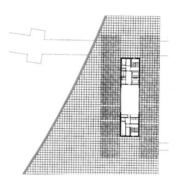

TRANSCO TOWER

Location	Houston, TX, USA
Architect	Johnson / Burgee Architects
Structural Engineer	CBM Engineers
Completion	1983
Height	275 m (902 ft)
Volume	ca 650 000 m³
Use	Office

Urban context

The building is located quite some distance from the city center of Houston and has already assumed an almost monumental role within the city's skyline – rather like the "steeple of a suburban village", as mentioned by John Burgee. Significantly taller than its neighbouring buildings, the structure dominates its surroundings both physically and conceptually, as it were; it stands on the outskirts of the city surrounded by freeways, hotels and supermarkets. On the south side of the building, Johnson had a park laid out in formal design, the lawn of which leads up to a pediment with three Roman arches.

The Transco Tower breaks with the conventional tradition of modern architecture, being anything but "International Style" in the sense of a Le Corbusier or Mies van der Rohe. In terms of expression it comes rather closer to Bertram Goodhue's modernistic State Capitol in Nebraska, which dates from 1916 and is an eclectic late work in Beaux-Arts style. Johnson, however, did not give this building a uniform design, but transformed the entrance into an enormous front panel framed by an 18 m-high portal composed of classical concrete elements. The contours of the Transco Tower feature projections and setbacks like those on a neo-gothic tower, with the crown of the battlement-like setbacks formed not by a flat roof but a flattened pyramidal finial.

Top of tower

Base of tower

Structure

The building has a steel skeleton and rests on a five-storey plinth. Its load-bearing structure comprises central cores into which the reinforcing walls are integrated. The columns are arranged along the façade, whereby the main part of the load is transferred via the set-back corners. The steel-and-glass façade structure is self-supporting.

Circulation / Installations

Access to the building is provided via a compact, centrally located core zone. The inner area, which is quite spacious in relation to the floor areas, comes as quite a surprise with its two stair-wells and almost twenty-five lifts, not to mention the installation shafts. Proceeding from the quadratic plan, diverse approaches have been provided for the individual office sections, thus permitting considerable flexibility in leasing floor space.

Façade

Although the building is fully glazed, its scale and colouring convey the impression of a stone structure. The mirrored panels are treated more like stone than glass. The extensive glass surfaces are separated by filigree mullions into units with dimensions normally used for stone-clad buildings. In this way the difference between glass and stone plates is dissolved. Contrasting with this is the gray filling of the vertical, V-formed projecting bays, which thus convey the effect of windows inserted between stone. The building exerts its most powerful impact in the evening, when the lighting merges with the glow of the sunset on the shimmering surface.

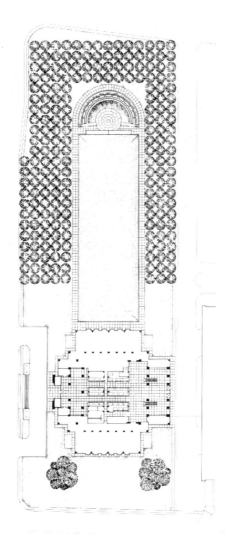

Site plan

Large bay-window section

61st floor

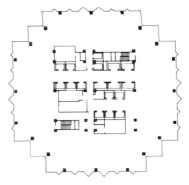

51st floor (sky lobby)

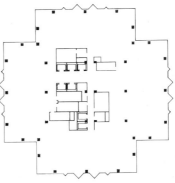

57th floor

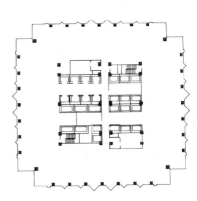

10th – 48th floor

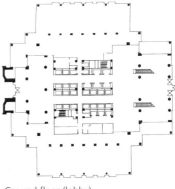

Ground floor (lobby)

121

TRUMP TOWER

Location	New York, NY, USA
Architect	Der Scutt of Swanke, Hayden, Connell Architects
Completion	1983
Height	210 m (688 ft)
Volume	ca 300 000 m³
Use	Shops, office, flats

Urban context

The 68-storey Trump Tower marks the corner of 5th Avenue and 57th Street and is a prominent example of mixed use by shops, offices and apartments. A special feature is the 10-m-wide ground-floor passage along its western side to the neighbouring IBM Building. This public pedestrian link runs along the inside of the street-side wall of Trump Towers. The passage is linked to a 6-storey atrium – open to the public – constructed as a glittering mirrored world with luxury shops. Another striking characteristic is the building's cascade-like, stepped plinth.

The Trump Tower is also one of the most complex zoning packages in the New York City. By making additional purchases and by securing the so-called "air rights" of the neighbouring Tiffany Company, Donald Trump, the developer, was able to increase the size of the plot (which had originally disposed of a usable floor area of 300 000 square feet) to an astonishing 756 000 square feet. With this clever investment trick, he not only sent his investment returns soaring, but also, as a welcome side effect, gained a view (which cannot be obstructed by further building) over the Tiffany Company towards Central Park and George Washington Bridge.

Structure

The building's load-bearing structure consists of a reinforced concrete structure. It is stiffened by the solid lift core and concrete slabs arranged in star formation.

Circulation / Installations

The core zone is located around the main access area comprising the staircase and four lifts at the centre of the ground plan. Together, three of the lifts and the emergency-escape staircase provide semi-public access to the tower. A fourth lift, located a little further away, transports goods. The building is air-conditioned.

Façade

The bronze-coloured curtain wall façade covering the reinforced concrete structure consists of a metal-frame in which the mirror-glass plates are set. The façade gives the building the appearance of a regular crystalline form. However, the building only really comes to life when it reflects the façade of the Crown Buildings. The "glass wall" makes it look as if the Trump Tower's own volume is dematerialised by the reflections of its surroundings.

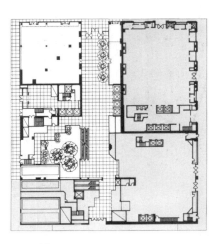

Ground floor

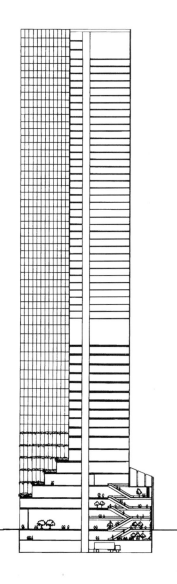

333 WACKER DRIVE

Location	Chicago, IL, USA
Architect	Kohn, Pedersen & Fox Associates
Completion	1983
Height	145 m (475 ft)
Volume	ca 350 000 m³
Use	Office

Urban context

Located where the street grid of the Loop encounters a bend in the river, the 36-storey building soars above the neighbouring buildings and fills the former gap at the south-east corner, setting a final accent. Its curved façade follows the bend in the river. A second façade and a forecourt face the Loop district.

Structure

The building, which is supported by columns, has a curtain-wall façade, which allowed the architects to freely use set-backs and projections on the façade. This approach also made it possible not only to define the tower volumetrically, but also to create a ground-floor arcade leading to the street area. The horizontal loads are absorbed by the centrally located core. The longitudinal design of the core determines the form of the two entrance lobbies, which are situated opposite one another on the ground floor.

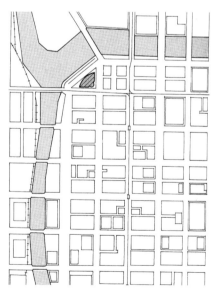

Site plan

Circulation / Installations

Both the vertical access and the piping are contained in the central core. There are three groups of lifts, each servicing a third of the floors. The entire first floor is taken up by the installations, evident in the large ventilation outlets in the façade facing the Loop. This is quite a sensible solution, since the E1 railway, parallel to the south side, runs at the same height, producing high levels of emission.

Façade

Clad in stone, the plinth stands out from the floors above it and thus establishes a relationship to the dimensions of the street area. The remainder of the façade is designed as a curtain wall. The choice of green for the fenestration takes up the colour of the river, whilst also reflecting the skyline opposite, depending on the light and weather. The horizontal plane has been rendered dynamic by curving the façade and accentuating the horizontal elements.

At the top, the façade is volumetrically proportioned with set-backs and projecting sections. The building as a whole is formed in accordance with classical vertical tripartitioning. Its exciting visual effect is based on the skilful staging of architectural resources such as geometry, the choice of materials and detail, combined with an acknowledgement and interpretation of essential elements in the surroundings. The triangular plot had lain waste for many years, and the developers gave much thought as to how this favourably situated yet awkwardly shaped plot could be filled to its advantage.

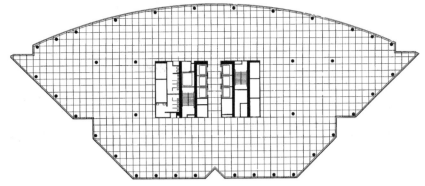

Typical storey

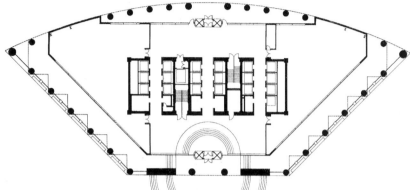

Ground floor

AT&T BUILDING

Location	New York, NY, USA
Architect	Johnson / Burgee Architects with Simons Architects
Structural Engineer	Skilling, Kelle, Christiansen & Robertson
Completion	1984
Height	197 m (646 ft)
Volume	ca 300 000 m³
Use	Shops, office

Urban context

The AT&T building, which now belongs to the Sony Group, is located at 550 Madison Avenue, between 55th and 56th Street, in Manhattan. Surrounded by a great number of skyscrapers, the building stands out because of its height, and, above all, its idiosyncratic formal language. The conspicuous gable-like crown, with its circular notch, confidently defies the modern convention of the flat-roof, thus defining the AT&T building as a unique part of the New York City skyline. The building, which critics have called the „Chippendale sky-scraper," played a major role in establishing Postmodernism. The inclusion of an arcade and a glass-covered shop passage, which was designed to link 55th and 56th Street, arose from Johnson's desire to integrate public space into the interior of the building.

Structure

As the zoning laws stipulated that shops had to be located on the ground floor, the entire building was raised 18 m above the ground and constructed on solid columns. This mode of support also made it possible to design an exceptionally high lobby and include the arcade. The wide columns taper towards the top. As elements of the steel skeleton structure, the two circulation cores serve to reinforce the building.

Circulation / Installations

The 37-storey AT&T Building has twenty-one lifts. Of these, however, only the service lift on the right side of the entrance hallway serves all floors. The so-called shuttle-lift opposite the entrance takes visitors from the entrance lobby to the sky-lobby on the first floor. Once they have arrived there, visitors can either change to the lifts located on the left to reach the floors in the lower half of the building, or take the lifts on the right if they want to ascend to any of the higher floors.

Façade

The façade is clad with unpolished pink granite. The articulation adopts the tripartition of the classical column. The central element of the plinth is the 35-m-high round-arched portal, which provides access to the spacious entrance and arcade areas. The rationally articulated shaft was consciously designed to accentuate the verticals. The perforated gable of the tower makes the building immediately recognisable on the New York skyline.

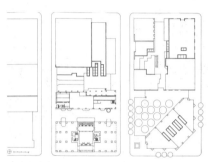

Site plan

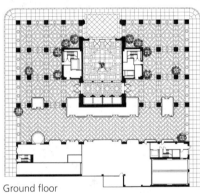

Ground floor

Lobby interior

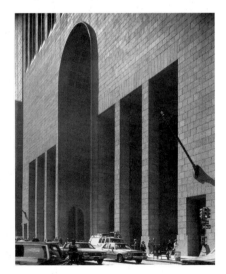

Entrance

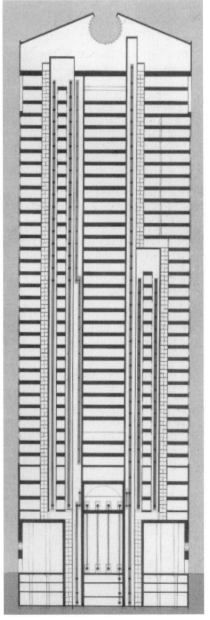

Section

127

MUSEUM OF MODERN ART RESIDENTIAL TOWER

Location	New York, NY, USA
Architect	Cesar Pelli & Associates
Structural Engineer	Rosenwasser & Associates
Completion	1984
Height	198 m (650 ft)
Volume	ca 170 000 m³
Use	Apartments

Urban context

The clear lines of this 53-storey tower – with its unique, visionary, tinted-glass façade – stand out against the densely developed surroundings like a work of art. The façade is reminiscent of a "Mondrian painting with plain areas and grids," and is regarded as a symbol of art itself.

On the occasion of its fiftieth anniversary, the Museum of Modern Art was planning to expand. As part of this plan, the existing exhibition space was to be doubled, the curatorial facilities enlarged, organisational procedures improved, and the bookshop and restaurant expanded to meet the demands created by the large number of visitors. However, in order to cover the operational deficit, the Museum decided on having a residential tower built above the new gallery.

Structure

The structure is based on a concrete skeleton with the lift and stairwell cores providing structural reinforcement. The span widths and dimensions are those normally found in skyscrapers used for residential apartments.

Circulation / Installations

Vertical circulation in the tower is provided by four lifts and an emergency staircase. The lift and stairwell cores are located in the tower centre and serve additionally to provide horizontal stability. Further shafts, primarily serving sanitation facilities to the apartments, are arranged in a circle around the lift core.

Façade

A complex composition of piers, tinted glass and eleven shades of parapet glass lend the façades of both the new tower and the museum building a unique appearance, which in terms of colour, pattern, and dimensions, corresponds to the surrounding urban area. For Pelli, an independent relationship between "skin" and "bones" is of great importance. He considers glass to be the only material suitable for a curtain-wall since it is the element with the least weight possible.

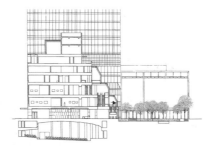

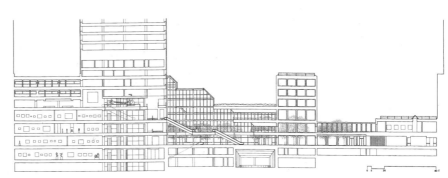

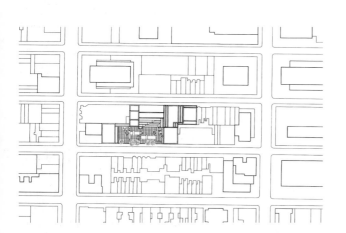

NATIONSBANK

Location   Houston, TX, USA

Architect   Johnson / Burgee Architects with
Kendall / Heaton & Associates

Structural   CBM Engineers, Inc.
Engineers

Completion   1984

Height   238 m (780 ft)

Volume   ca 580 000 m³

Use   Bank, office

Urban context

The NationsBank (previously Repub-
licBank or NCNB) is located in the
commercial district of Houston.
Nestling between two high-rise structures aligned with the street, the complex occupies a full block site. The
bank is divided into two buildings –
the 12-storey banking hall integrating
a concealed single-storey building that
previously occupied the site, and the
56-storey office tower. This spatial
composition creates a very succinct
Urban context. The 4-storey plinth
zone of the office tower reaches the
height of the banking hall, creating a
link between the tower and the latter
structure. The office tower features
two pronounced setbacks, which
relate to the dimensions of the urban
surroundings.
Formally reminiscent of Amsterdam
town houses, with their narrow, high
gables, this building – so rich in allu-
sion – is yet another highlight in the
phase of postmodernist skyscraper
design inaugurated by Philip Johnson
with his AT&T building.

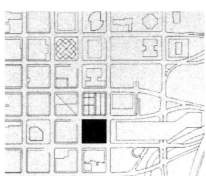

Site plan

130

Structure

The office tower is a steel skeleton structure with centrally located cores serving to transfer the horizontal and the shear stresses, whilst the vertical forces are transferred by the columns. The banking hall is a reinforced concrete structure. The columns are clad in granite slabs and the roof is composed of a network of vaults and columns.

Circulation / Installations

The building has six lift groups flanked by installation and ventilation shafts (a total of ten lifts and four stairwells). Air circulation within the building is controlled by a central air-conditioning system within the cooling tower.

Façade

Having a distinct plinth zone, a middle zone and a roof zone the form of the façade is based on traditional design principles. The roof zone of the tower is, in turn, also divided into a middle zone and a roof zone. The upper section is formed by obelisks and set-backs, creating a filigree effect. By contrast, due to its stone sheathing, the plinth zone appears extremely solid and static. The tower has a highly textured façade, creating an effect of depth. The relief-like rhythmic structure of corners, entrances, granite ribs and mullions gives the façade sculptural quality. Both the banking hall and the office tower have a curtain-wall façade. The banking hall is sheathed in granite and the tower in painted aluminium.

Banking hall

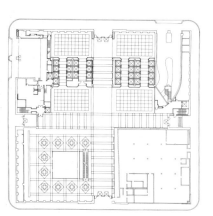

Ground floor plan

Façade

Section showing skylights

ATLANTA MARRIOTT MARQUIS

Location	Atlanta, GA, USA
Architect	John Portman & Associates
Structural Engineer	John Portman & Associates
Completion	1985
Height	170 m (557 ft)
Volume	ca 500 000 m³
Use	Hotel

Urban context

Portmann establishes a relationship with the two hotels standing close by: the Westin Peachtree Plaza Hotel and the Hyatt Regency. He achieves this by placing the hotel asymmetrically to the existing hotels and using the intermediate space to create a semi-public plaza in front of the hotel entrance. The three hotels are prime examples of the transformations architectural design philosophy has undergone during the past twenty years. The hotel, with its 1 675 rooms, is subdivided by a dramatic atrium rising fifty floors above the lobby. The lobby, in turn, is divided into an upperzone housing restaurants, lounges and a swimming pool, and a lower level accommodating the registration desk, a ballroom, convention centres and meeting rooms. Vertically, the hotel is effectively divided into private and public zones. The circulation areas situated at different levels give the very urbane interior a spacious and novel atmosphere. Portmann's hotels, with their playfully creative elements, have done much to make Atlanta into an attractive cosmopolitan city that draws people travelling on business as well as sports enthusiasts en masse.

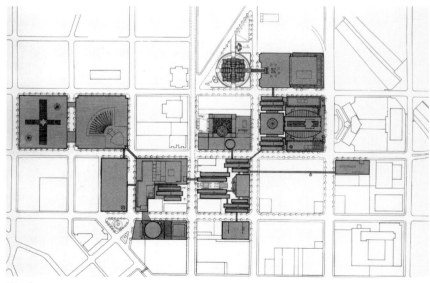

Site plan

132

Structure

The almost elliptical form of the hotel tower is born by cross walls and two external staircases. Two "supporting levels" have been created by variations in the ground plan. The interior lift shaft reinforces the structure.

Circulation / Installations

The elevators to the rooms are located in the round load-bearing inner core, whilst the stairs ascend in the exterior, asymmetrically arranged cores. Based on a four-storey design, the tower is subdivided into three zones for functional purposes. Each zone is supplied on both sides with service rooms.

Façade

The load-bearing structure makes the tower appear almost conical from the outside. The cross walls add vertical rhythm to the outer articulation of the north and south façades and to the external cores of the east and west elevations.

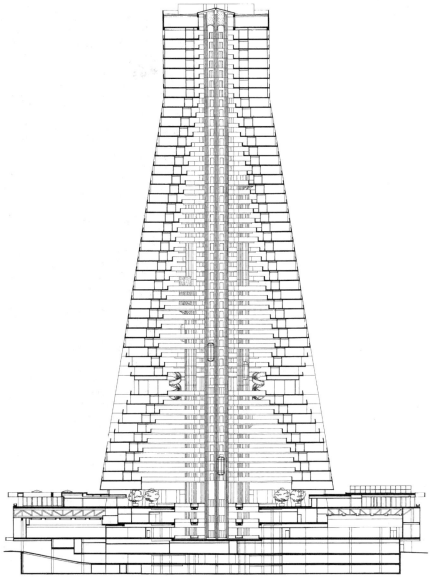

Cross section

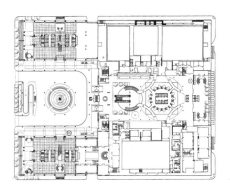

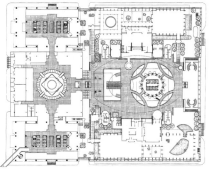

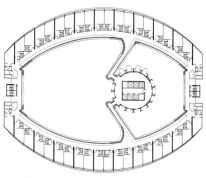

Typical room storey

HONG KONG & SHANGHAI BANK

Location	Hong Kong, China
Architect	Norman Foster & Partners
Structural Engineers	Ove Arup & Partners
Completion	1985
Height	180 m (590 ft)
Volume	ca 300 000 m³
Use	Bank

Urban context

The Hong Kong & Shanghai Bank is located on one of the most splendid sites in Hong Kong's business centre and stands in a direct line with the Star Ferry Terminal. Between the bank and the harbour, there is a park and a multi-storey car park. The classical style of the existing law-court building (directly neighbouring the Hong Kong and Shanghai Bank) offers the most striking contrast to the bank. The bank tower emphasises the importance of both the Chinese-British territory of Hong Kong and the company itself – the foremost bank in the Far East and Hong Kong's central bank – within the international financial world. As an institution and symbol, the Hong Kong and Shanghai Bank expresses the confidence placed in the future of Hong Kong. The ground-floor access area to the bank is interesting in terms of urban context: a public space has been created by allowing the public to traverse the building. From lower level, escalators lead to the bank's enormous, internal atrium.

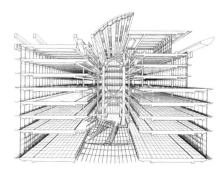

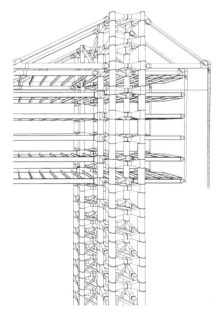

Structure

The vertical loads are transferred by a total of eight columns of cantilever transfer structures in combination with hangers. Together with the diagonals and verticals providing reinforcement tension, they form the dominant features of the façade. Horizontal loads are absorbed by reinforcing storeys.

Circulation / Installations

In designing this building, the aim was to create extensive unified areas and thus achieve transparency and maximum flexibility. For this reason, nearly all the vertical structural elements, as well as the circulation and service shafts, are arranged on the building's external skins. The cores are located in the east and west façades. Vertical movement is provided by a combination of express lifts, with central escalators for local circulation. The form of the building reflects the circulation density, which decreases towards the top.

Façade

Foster's magnificent building represents a new aesthetic, which no longer distinguishes between the science of engineering and the "art" of architecture. The façade design demonstrates how the structure itself can become ornamentation and the structural principle a stylistic device. In designing the building, Foster drew on the principles underlying suspension bridges, which make an internal supporting structure superfluous.

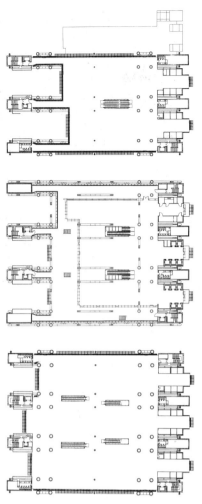

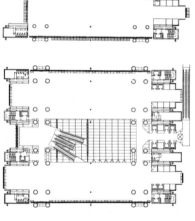

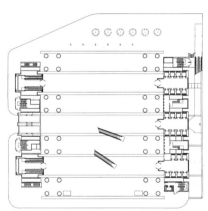

Ground floor

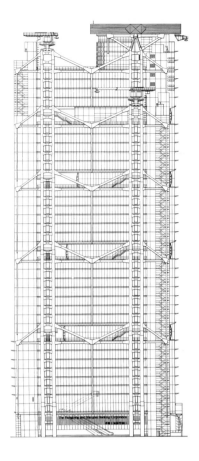

WORLD FINANCIAL CENTER

Location   New York, NY, USA

Architect   Cesar Pelli & Associates

Structural   M.S. Yolles & Partners
Engineer

Completion   1985

Height   120–225 m (393–739 ft)

Volume   ca 3 000 000 m³ (entire complex)

Use   Shops, hotel, office

Urban context

The World Financial Center is located on the bank of the Hudson River. The towers of the World Trade Center rise up behind it. Built on land originally reserved for a government-subsidised housing project, the World Financial Center complex stands as a symbol of the end of the "seventies" recession. The ensemble is a multi-functional complex consisting of four high-rise towers with thirty-seven to fifty-one floors, a winter garden, three public squares and two 9-storey buildings. Buildings B, C and D (original position) call to mind the layout of court in which the missing building – A – is occupied by a public square. The square touches the riverbank diagonally, giving the ensemble direct access to both the Hudson riverside and the ocean.

Buildings A and B (new position) have been set back from their original position and, together, form a gateway, which is consciously accentuated by the positioning of the two 9-storey buildings.

The four towers function like six buildings, of which building B performs a dual role. Although an essential part of the court composition, it simultaneously serves as an element of the gateway. Between buildings B and C there is a glass pavilion, and between C and D a large hall.

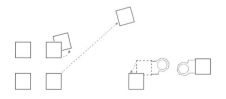

Structure

The buildings constituting the World Financial Center stand on a common plinth built around a steel frame reinforced by vertical access shafts.

Circulation / Installations

The lifts and installations are located in the cores of the single towers. A central equipment room is housed in the basement.

Façade

The façade is composed of granite and reflecting glass. The four glazed main towers rise from a continuous granite plinth. Granite slabs, which are used to clad the lower storeys, gradually give way to glass higher up. Glass predominates on the top sections of the buildings. The towers are crowned by massive roofs.

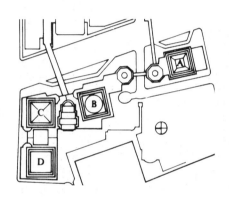

Model

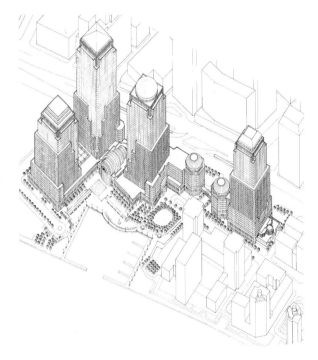

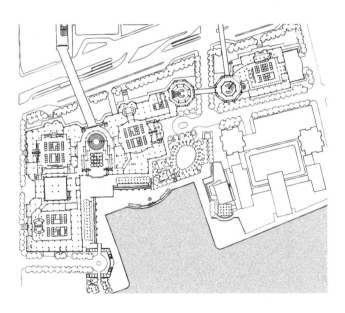

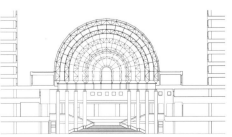

ALLIED BANK BUILDING

Location	Dallas, TX, USA
Architect	Henry Cobb of Pei, Cobb, Freed
Completed	1986
Height	219 m (718 ft)
Volume	ca 410 000 m³
Use	Bank, office

Urban context

As the Allied Bank Tower is located on the edge of the city's commercial district, the developer wanted a striking building that could be easily leased, despite its somewhat peripheral location. Its impressive geometry is based on a square measuring 58.50 m x 58.50 m, above which a parallelogram rises to a soaring gabled crown. These two basic forms are linked by prismatic intermediate elements with inclined outer surfaces.

A pedestrian zone, whose tasteful design makes abundant use of water, was created on the ground floor to stand out against the surroundings, which are characterised by car parks, down-market shops and a freeway. In this way, the architect wanted to establish a point of reference in a rather drab environment. There are plans to supplement the tower with a hotel as well as a second building, identical in form, but turned at an angle of ninety degrees to the first one.

Structure

The entire load-bearing structure had to be located in the tubular skin of the façades, since the dimensions of the core area change considerably with the height of the building. A structure was chosen, similar to that employed for the John Hancock Center in Chicago, based on a close network of diagonal elements, with a relatively large distance between the external columns.

The tubular skin functions as a 40-storey "mega-truss" composed of eight "sub-trusses" placed on top of one another. Horizontal girders in a Vierendeel-truss structure link the truss to the vertexes of the diagonals. The gable above the forty-fifth floor is created by a Vierendeel-truss system, with columns positioned at close intervals in the façade.

Circulation / Installations

The conventional lift shaft is divided into three vertical zones. Located along the central axis of the parallelogram, it has been constructed to taper toward the top of the building.

Façade

The building claims to be the highest in the world to use silicon glazing fully bonded to interior glazing bars. The panels, flush on all sides, are made of green, shimmering solar glass, and are only linked by a thin joint grid, thus creating a graphic impact. Consequently, the building resembles an abstract, minimalist sculpture whose appearance constantly changes whatever angle it is viewed from.

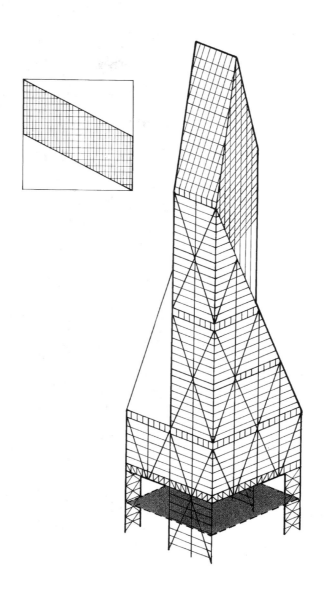

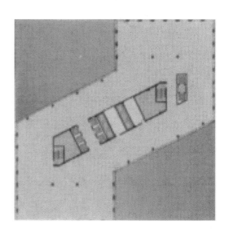

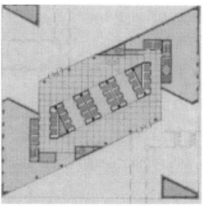

LIPSTICK BUILDING

Location	New York, NY, USA
Architect	Johnson / Burgee Architects
Structural Engineer	The Office of Irwin G. Kantor
Completion	1986
Height	133 m (436 ft)
Volume	ca 160 000 m³
Use	Office

Urban context

Situated at the corner of 53rd Street and 5th Avenue, the Lipstick Building is a complex comprising a 33-storey elliptical office building and a 6-storey rectangular extension, whose impact fades in view of the dominance, form and height of the main building. With its elliptical ground plan, the building breaks with the quadratic grid form, thus creating a dramatic contrast to the neighbouring buildings, all based on a strictly quadratic grid. Architect Philip Johnson tersely referred to it as an oval building in a rectangular environment. Apart from the clarity of the idea underlying its unusual form, the building was also the architect's response to the Zoning Laws (three set-backs in accordance with the development plan) and the atmosphere on a densely built-up 3rd Avenue. Its conspicuous shape has made the Lipstick Building into one of the best-known skyscrapers in New York. It was affectionately baptised the "Lipstick" building even prior to its official opening.

The vast entrance hall, designed in postmodernist style, is a surprise in itself, and seems to be far too large for the building as viewed from the outside.

Structure

The reinforced concrete structure consists of an inner core, which houses all the installations and vertical access links, and a ring of external columns. Horizontal loads are transferred into the core via the storey floors.

Circulation / Installations

The fourteen lifts and two emergency-escape staircases are located in the rear of the building.
Their decentralised position creates maximum floor area for the landlords on New York's financially attractive 3rd Avenue.

Façade

The curtain-wall façade is characterised by its succession of alternating horizontal bands of enamelled and fired granite, narrow and wide stainless steel, and grey-tinted strip windows. The smooth, rounded façade has thus been adorned with almost every element of postmodernist historical ornamentation featured by Johnson's other buildings over the past decade.

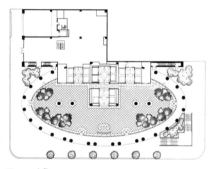

Ground floor

LLOYD'S BUILDING

Location	London, Great Britain
Architect	Richard Rogers & Partners
Structural Engineer	Ove Arup & Partners
Completion	1986
Height	87 m (285 ft)
Volume	ca 150 000 m³
Use	Services, office

Urban context

Richard Rogers found a unique solution to the complex requirements of the insurance company. He designed a structure on a rectangular plan including a central atrium with a completely open ground floor, whilst locating the entire vertical access as well as the service systems and rooms on the exterior of the building in six independent service towers. The complex is six to twelve storeys high and is surrounded by lower buildings of some historical interest. The proportions and finely executed details skilfully help the building blend into its contrasting, medieval, urban surroundings. The Lloyd's Building is a product of the fashion, then prevalent, for high-tech machine aesthetics.

Structure

The structure is a prefabricated double stress system in reinforced concrete, with inverted U-beams to transfer the floor loads onto the outer cylindrical columns. A separate pre-fabricated strut linked to the cylindrical columns solved the problem of connecting the beams and the cylindrical columns. A second pre-fabricated element transfers the load from the U-beams to the struts. The concrete columns run the entire height of the atrium up to the barrel vault. They constitute the main supports for the circular steel frame.

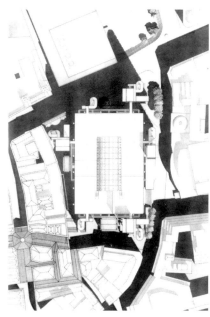

Site plan

142

Circulation / Installations

Placing the entire functional areas on the exterior of the building is a literal interpretation of the serving and served areas as understood by Louis Kahn. The installations, neatly packed in silver boxes on top of the towers, have an irresistible functional and architectural logic. The glazing serves as a technical wall, not only keeping out wind and rain, but also functioning as both an air-shaft and insulation. Air passes from beneath the ceiling to the ground floor via the space between the double external glazing and the single second skin.

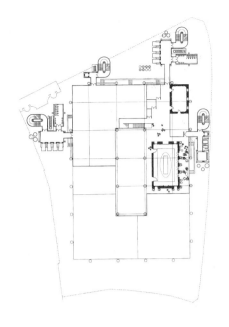 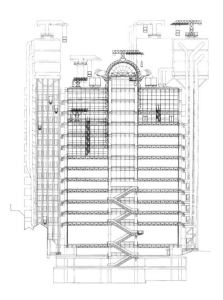

Façade

The extremely smooth surface of the visible concrete structure was achieved using cast plastic-coated sections. The stairwells, the entire lining, the pipe sleeves and the silver boxes on the towers are clad in stainless steel; aluminium was used for the window frames. The atrium frame is made of stainless steel.

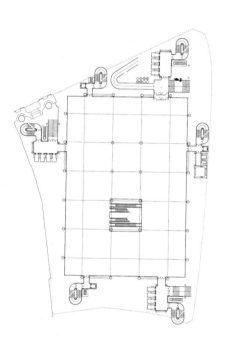 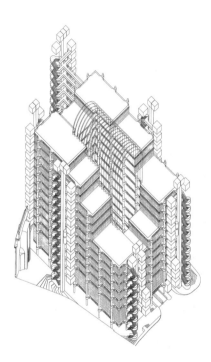

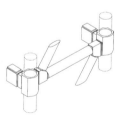

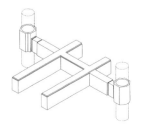

OUB CENTRE

Location	Singapore
Architect	Kenzo Tange & Associates
Structural Engineer	W.L. Meinhardt & Partners
Completion	1986
Height	280 m (919 ft)
Volume	ca 450 000 m³
Use	Bank, stock exchange, office

Urban context

The Overseas Union Bank (OUB) is located in Singapore's financial centre. The plinth of the tower establishes a relationship with Raffles Place, whose subterranean level contains the central underground connection. Raffles Place, which is to be developed as a green area, and the OUB Tower constitute the core of the Singapore development zone. Situated below the tower is the prestigious bank lobby, whose 36-m-high entrance area creates a vista taking in the OUB, Raffles Place and Singapore River. The building is subdivided into two clearly distinguished volumes: a lower and a higher tower standing back-to-back. Each tower stands on a triangular plan. A particularly impressive feature is the entrance with its almost 40-m-high atrium providing an exciting view of the surrounding area.

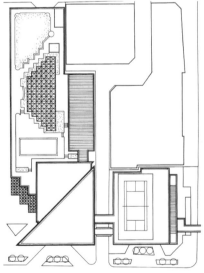

Site plan

144

Structure

The plinth and the secondary building are constructed around a supporting structure. The tower, the plan of which measures 28 m x 41.50 m, was erected as a clear-span structure made possible by using a steel-beam floor with an estimated static height of 1.25 m. The reinforcing elements are located in triangular corners in the top floor zone; from the upper to the lower floors they are concentrated in the four corners of the tower.

Circulation / Installations

The entire complex has twenty-nine lifts; the supply shafts being located in the stairwells. The tower is supplied with a part of the necessary technical services on five double storeys. The aggregate exchange at the equipment floors is carried out along the façade by means of a swing-out crane.

Façade

The single tower sections, between which an equipment floor is located, are legible on the façade. The curtain wall of steel, aluminium and glass accentuates the elegance of the building. The colour of the chemically processed aluminium sheeting of the outer skin varies in accordance with changes in the reflected light. With its simple and elegant design, the OUB Tower enhances the continually changing face of Singapore in a pleasing and unforgettable manner.

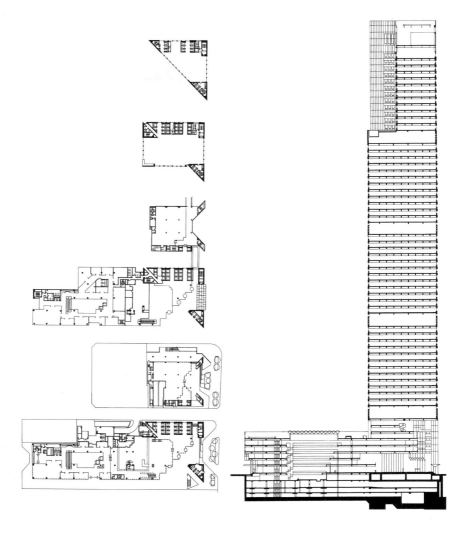

LIPPO CENTER

Location   Hong Kong, China

Architect   Paul M. Rudolph

Completion   1988

Height   ca 150 m (490 ft)

Volume   ca 300 000 m³

Use   Office

Urban context

The Lippo Center, formerly known as the Bond Center, stands in the heart of the Central District. It consists of two octagonal towers of thirty-six and forty storeys respectively, rising over a 4-storey disc-shaped plinth, which contains the distribution centre. Vertically, both towers are divided into three sections. The projecting storeys (the Sky Rooms) at the end of each section give this building its unique character. The projecting storeys extend beyond the central structure and are facetted, allowing corner windows on many floors.

Structure

Like almost all very high buildings, the vertical load-bearing system of these towers is extremely simple and consists of two individual, appropriately connected systems: a central core and a number of piers placed in front of the façade. The twelve largest supporting round piers are made of reinforced concrete, poured on site in segments of two meters in diameter, and symmetrically arranged around the central core. Some of the piers are entirely enclosed in the external skin, whilst others are partly visible up to varying heights before vanishing into the façade of this impressive structure. The horizontal load-bearing system is largely determined by the projecting sections. Irrespective of its form, each storey consists of up to eight façade elements, with four short and four long ones, thus providing the maximum number of corner windows.

146

Circulation / Installations

The architecture of the lower plinth storeys has been lightened by a series of stairs, loggias, verandas, terraces, and foyers, which are designed like small plazas to lend the interior of the building that open atmosphere characteristic of its urban surroundings. These variously designed circulation areas lead to the entrance hall, the central point of the complex, which provides vertical access. Underneath, a subway station links the area with the rest of the city.

Floor diagrams

Façade

Both towers are completely clad in reflecting glass. Glass, when used for façades, guarantees considerable structural resistance against strong wind loads and is air- and watertight. The expansive façade facing the ocean bay allows a magnificent view and enhances the Hong Kong skyline.

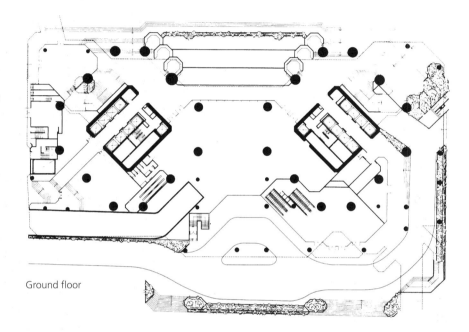

Ground floor

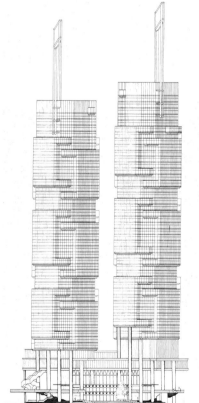

MILLENIUM TOWER

Location	Tokyo, Japan
Architect	Norman Foster & Partners
Structural Engineer	Obayashi Corporation
Project	1989
Height	840 m (2 754 ft)
Volume	ca 3 700 000 m³
Use	Multifunctional skyscraper

Urban context

Foster was commissioned by the Japanese Obayashi group of companies to carry out a study into the possibilities and effects of a building complex standing alone in the sea, or more specifically: in Tokyo Bay. The complex was to have its own independent urban statics as a vertical city of 50 000 inhabitants.

Foster's design envisaged a causeway and a mole around the base of the tower. They were to establish a visual relationship between the verticality of the skyscraper and the horizontal expanse of the ocean, whilst the sudden change in the character of the natural surroundings would surprise visitors approaching by car, train or boat. Formally, the tower is a free-standing structure without an axial relationship to the mole.

Structure

The Millenium Tower is a tube-in-tube structure consisting of an outer cone and a slender supply core. In trials made with various structural forms to test wind bracing and earthquake resistance, the conical form proved to be the most favourable, especially with regard to building costs and construction time.

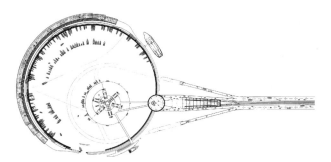

Site plan

148

Circulation / Installations

Inside the tower, there is a central supply core providing technical services and access, which is either by express lift or slower local lifts. The upper two-sevenths of the tower are open and designed to accommodate solar and wind energy collectors, among other things.

Façade

At first glance, the tower seems very compact. Its conical form flattens the lattice of the external bearing structure at the lower levels, whilst intensifying it towards the top. This use of dynamic lines adds emphasis to the shape of the building. When approaching the tower, one notices the "sinews" of the external structure with their alternating closed and open surfaces. The transparent cladding reveals the heterogeneous space within the tower, thus dispelling all notions of an "isolated island" from the very start.

Typical storey

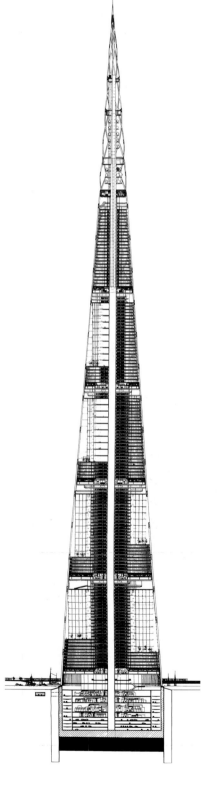

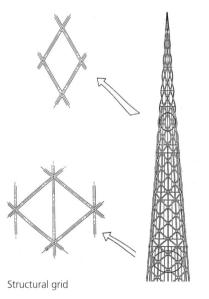

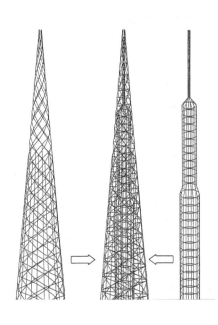

Structural grid

NORWEST CENTER

Location	Minneapolis, MN, USA
Architect	Cesar Pelli & Associates with Kendall/Heaton Architects
Structural Engineer	CBM Engineers
Completion	1988
Height	236 m (773 ft)
Volume	ca 800 000 m³
Use	Office

Urban context

The Norwest Tower owes its present-day appearance to a somewhat unhappy circumstance: After the former headquarters of the bank burned down in 1982, the management set about planning a large building complex over the entire block. The various parties involved, however, failed to reach agreement, so that the bank then concentrated on its own part of the site. The new rectangular form represented an exciting and impressive solution in the heart of the most important district in Minneapolis. The design represents an attempt at a cautious approach towards a postmodernist architectural language; reviving the charisma and grandeur of the skyscrapers of the nineteen-thirties and -forties without attempting to adopt too literally the formal language of those times. The result "reflects the past but doesn't lie about the fact that it is new". The overall design can be seen as a tribute to Hood's RCA Building in New York, where the celebration of verticality was employed in an irresistible manner.

The interior design took up many of the features of the gutted building, such as chandeliers, cast rails, sculptured bronze plaques, and commemorative medallions, thus preserving its old spirit.

Structure

The structure follows customary practices with its central reinforcing core and load-bearing columns along the perimeter.

Circulation / Installations

Access to the building on the ground floor is via twenty-eight lifts grouped in cross formation around the central, rectangular core area. A multi-storey, zenith-lit rotunda, projecting from the plinth structure on 6th Street, creates a reception area worthy of the bank. The building contains state-of-the-art technical equipment. For obvious reasons, particular emphasis was placed on fire precautions inside the building: A complete sprinkler system, smoke extraction devices, fire-resistant emergency staircases, fire-service lifts, and an excellently equipped fire management centre have been installed to protect the bank from a further loss of US$ 100 million in future.

Façade

The 57-storey Norwest Tower is set back gradually with increasing height. Rising from a solid granite plinth, it rises to a bright crown of glass and marble. The building skin is made of Minnesota amber stone, a golden-hued material also common in many downtown buildings, and thin vertical bands and accents of white marble. Together, the two materials evoke a warmth that is very welcome during the long winters.

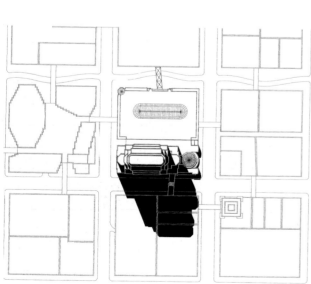

Site plan

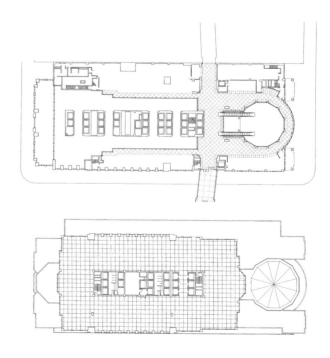

TOUR SANS FIN

Location	Paris, France
Architect	Jean Nouvel & Partners
Project	1989
Height	420 m (1377 ft)
Volume	ca 600 000 m³
Use	Office

Urban context

The triangular plot on which the Tour sans Fin is to be erected is surrounded by three traffic axes. It is located in the La Défence area between La Grande Arche de la Défense and le C.N.I.T. With its simple immateriality, the tower design represents the antithesis of the geometrical style of most of the buildings surrounding it. On the one hand, Nouvel has the foundation disappear, so that the tower seems to rise up out of a crater; on the other hand, the structure appears to become lighter and lighter as it ascends and even to dissolve into nothing at the top. The Tour sans Fin faces the Eiffel Tower as one expression of a vertical conception, whilst refusing to embody anything other than its function as receptacle for offices of various kinds.

Structure

As the tower, with a diameter of 43 m, does not allow for any core structure due to the horizontal loads, the load-bearing structure has been shifted to the periphery.

The base is constructed of normal concrete. The glazed area only accounts for 50% of the surface on the lowest storeys. Towards the top of the building, the rung-structure becomes lighter, before finally giving way to a fine metal structure on the top floors. In order to reduce the span, a ring of supports has been placed in the centre of the radial plan. On the transfer floors, this ring is replaced by columns integrated into the service shafts. Hence, the structure leaves the entire enclosed space free.

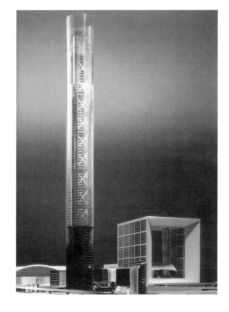

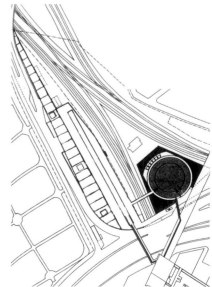

Circulation / Installations

The installations are housed in the periphery to keep the inner core free. The same applies to the circulation: slow lifts ascend and descend on the inner side and express lifts on the outer side of the façade. A strict distinction is made between public and private zones. Some of the transfer floors are equipped with escalators.

Façade

The circular tower is designed be nothing other than a simple, smooth building. The subtle use of materials has allowed the creation of a building that appears to be infinite. Dark at the bottom, the façade becomes brighter towards the top. Rough granite gives way to polished granite followed by grey stone, succeeded in turn by glass, which is screen printed with ever-greater intensity towards the top of the building, where it finally creates the impression of total immateriality. The transfer and office floors alternate at regular intervals. The visual impact of a graduated change in height is enhanced by the use of different kinds of glass.

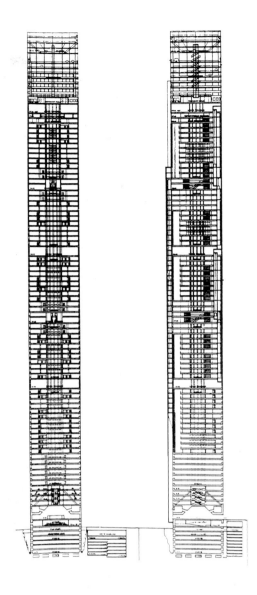

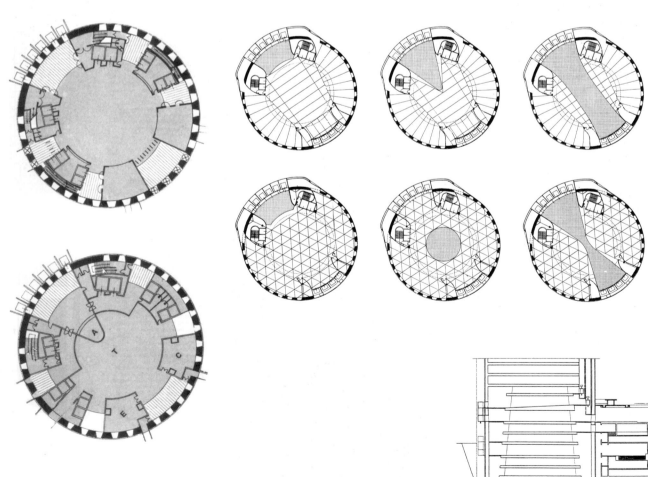

Plinth structure

BANK OF CHINA

Location	Hong Kong, China
Architect	I.M. Pei & Partners
Structural Engineers	Robertson, Fowler & Associates
Completion	1990
Height	369 m (1210 ft)
Volume	ca 500 000 m³
Use	Bank, office

Urban context

The Bank of China stands on a small, steeply sloping plot in the middle of the densely populated main commercial district of Hong Kong. The 0.8-hectare plot is almost completely surrounded by a tangled network of motorways, expressways and motorway exits, making access difficult. Being the tallest building in the district, and occupying the most central location, it dominates the skyline and seems to be China's answer to what was then still a British colony, especially since the developer was the People's Republic of China. Inside the monumental granite plinth surrounding the first three floors, one finds courtyards and ornamental waterworks in the midst of this traffic jungle. They constitute a small and almost intimate island very reminiscent of Chinese gardens, providing a constant contrast between the hustle and bustle of the city outside the building and the peaceful atmosphere within.

Critics objected to the triangular ground-plan forms, pointing out that the building neglected Chinese Feng Shui principles and traditions, which avoids acute angles as they disturb the yin-yang balance. However, since the Chinese Government did not recognise these principles, the tower was constructed as planned.

Structure

According to Pei, the model for the diagonal load-bearing structure, which is visible from the outside, was a simplified version of traditional Chinese bamboo framework. The horizontal forces are transferred through the rein-

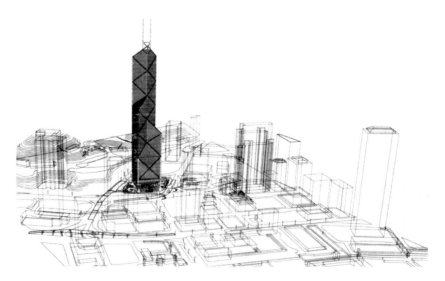

forced concrete trusses in the façade to the ceilings, where they are absorbed by four solid concrete piers and then transferred vertically. Wind speeds are very high in Hong Kong, and these concrete piers absorb most of these forces, too. The vertical forces and the permanent load of the floors are transferred vertically through the steel skeleton and the concrete lift and circulation shafts.

Circulation / Installations

Two diagonals divide the quadratic ground plan into four segments, each of which rises to a different height, thus lending the building its diamond-like shape. The number of lifts (twenty-four in the plinth section) diminishes towards the top of the building. In the extended sections, the lifts ascend to the top of the building. The stairs and the ducts for the technical installations, which also rise through the centre of the building, form – together with the lifts – the building core proper and link the seventy floors. Smaller shafts, linking a few floors only and located at the periphery of the building, supplement the main shafts.

Façade

The fields of the reinforced steel truss framework on the outside of the building are filled with a flush steel-glass structure. The façade and the skeleton form a flush surface. The façade forms a part of the light-coloured load-bearing structure (and vice versa), thus creating a marked contrast to the dark glazing.

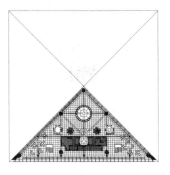

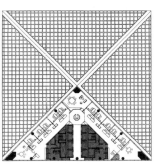

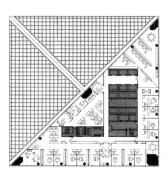

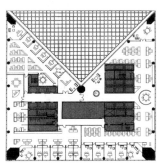

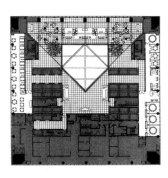

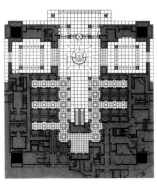

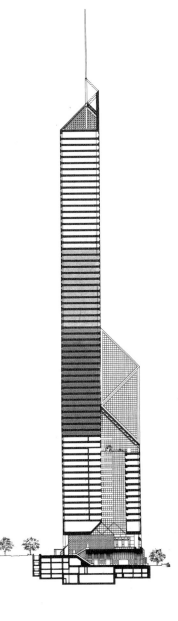

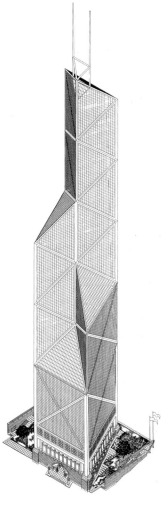

FIRST INTERSTATE
WORLD CENTER

Location	Los Angeles, CA, USA
Architect	Pei Cobb Freed & Partners
Structural Engineer	CBM Engineers
Completion	1990
Height	310 m (1 017 ft)
Volume	ca 550 000 m³
Use	Bank, offices

Urban context

Anyone viewing the First Interstate World Center would gain the impression of a slender and elegant landmark standing among the most diversely designed skyscrapers in downtown Los Angeles. Seen closer up, however, the building not only loses some of its dominance but also some of its clearly defined presence within the street environment due to the obscure design of the plinth and the uniform treatment of its glass-granite façade. From the ground plan to the design of the façade, the 75-storey-high tower is organised around a geometric plan of overlapping circles and rectangles.

Structure

The load-bearing structure of the tower, which is located in an area exposed to severe earthquakes, consists of two structural elements: a rigid core and a ductile outer skin. As the core structure absorbs the greater part of the loads and horizontal forces, the corner columns have been constructed of hollow poured-steel sections. Up to the fifty-third floor, the earthquake and wind loads are absorbed by two, storey-high struts. Higher up, however, the core is composed of reinforced quadrangular frames. The ductile edge zone, which does not have to perform a load-bearing function, was designed with a variety of set-backs.
The building has been constructed to withstand earthquake tremors of up to 8.3 on the Richter scale.

Circulation / Installations

The circulation areas comprise a concentrated core zone with some twenty-two lifts, two fire-escape staircases and the installation shafts. The support-free office areas can be reached by the shortest distance via cross-shaped circulation routes. This ingenious arrangement allows great flexibility in arranging the office areas, which can be easily separated from one another without inhibiting access.

Façade

The façade, which is composed of a system of light granite slabs and glass plates, is linked to the core by 20-m concrete slabs. Although the façade cannot, therefore, transfer considerable loads, it is able to absorb earthquake-induced deformation of up to five centimetres per floor without any danger of destruction.

Skyscrapers appear to us as symbols of greatness, power and endurance. The First Interstate World Center is probably the first tower that was forced to "witness" its own total, virtual destruction. In the film Independence Day, released in 1997, it was one of the buildings to be destroyed by alien invaders.

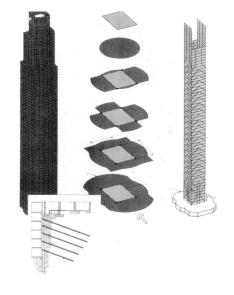

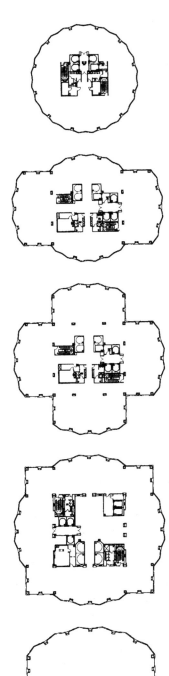

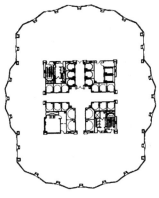

Floor schemes

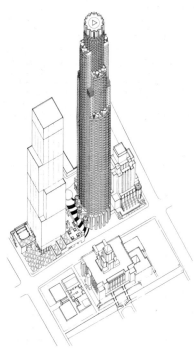

Axonometric view

INTERNATIONAL PLACE

Location	Boston, MA, USA
Architects	Johnson / Burgee Architects
Completion	I: 1987
	II: 1990
Height	ca 160 m (525 ft)
Volume	ca 700 000 m³
Use	Office, public functions

Urban context

In order to cope with the problems created by the irregular triangular plot – a legacy of Boston's historical street plan – an architectural composition has been created which fits harmoniously into the surrounding urban area. Grouped around a public plaza are variously shaped buildings, both cylindrical and rectangular. The uniqueness of the plot shape is respected by using the cylindrical form as the rounded corners of the buildings, and because the street front remains complete, the characteristic impression of the whole site is intensified. The use of the circle as a main formal element on the ground floor repeats this motif in a deliberately conspicuous way. The cylinder and rectangle are both opposed and connected to each other, yet the heights used are different. According to the architects Johnson and Burgee, this creates carefully established balance for the superstructure, thus sensitively fusing the buildings both optically and materially into an architecturally connected urban complex of structures. The primary means used to achieve this aim is the cylinder, since it lends the complex of buildings depth, contrast and variety.

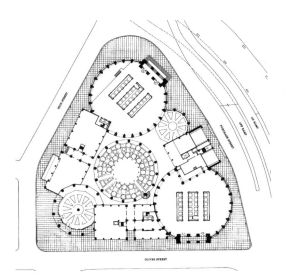

Site plan

Structure

In both towers, the main load-bearing structure consists of the centrally situated loft core together with the load-bearing columns of the façade; the lift core simultaneously serves as a reinforcing element. The support structure in the cubic shapes is made up of the load-bearing columns in the façade and internal supports with supporting walls throughout as reinforcement.

Circulation / Installations

Vertical access in the two circular towers consists of twenty-two passenger lifts and one goods lift, which together provide systematic access to all individual floors. The office storeys are provided with conventional air-conditioning.

Façade

Each element of the complex is clad in natural stone and has windows flush with the façade. The use of an almost ornamental design for the windows of the three cubic buildings creates a sharp contrast to the geometrical structured façade of the two towers. The entrances to the towers are especially emphasised by their size, since, at these points, the façade runs parallel to the street line and breaks out of the circular form. Both of the circular entrance pavilions leading to the courtyard are set off against the larger buildings through the contrast in material and colour.

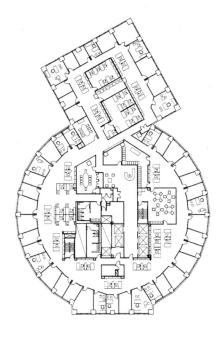

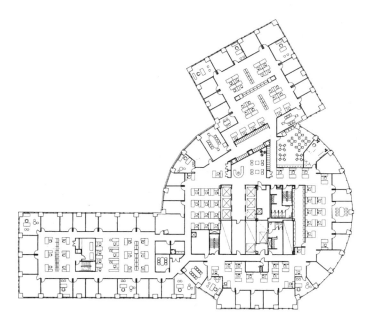

MESSETURM

Location	Frankfurt, Germany
Architects	Murphy / Jahn, Inc.
Structural Engineers	F. Noetzold, the Office of I.G. Cantor
Completion	1990
Height	257 m (843 ft)
Volume	ca 350 000 m³
Use	Office

Urban context

As one of Europe's highest buildings, there is a certain logic behind the fact that the Messeturm was erected in Frankfurt, one of the few European cities in which high-rise buildings are not merely tolerated on the periphery, or as single objects in the city centre, but where this type of structure has been used throughout the central area of the city. Even so, the positioning of the towers contradicts the original plan, which only permitted high-rise buildings in a single street and on the site of the former railway station. Being located next to the entry pavillion and the new Exhibition Hall 1 and not least on account of its gate-like plinth, the Messeturm emphasizes the "City Gateway" – the new exhibition complex entrance directing visitors into the city centre.

As a carefully designed classical composition the Messeturm is defined by a plinth, shaft and entablature.

Structure

The reinforced concrete forms the primary bearing structure and wind bracing. For the exterior façade, reinforced concrete was also used as the load-bearing element, which, particularly during the construction phase, created the impression of a punctuated façade.

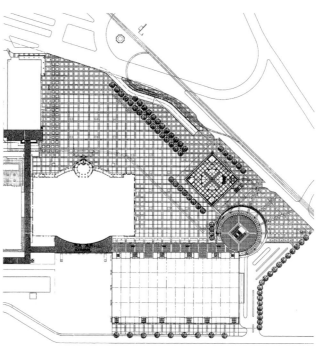

Site plan

160

Circulation / Installations

All the technical equipment servicing the different storeys, as well as the twenty passenger express lifts and two goods lifts, are located in the core. The main technical equipment is located on the first floor, in the pyramid at the top of the building and on the floor directly below.

Façade

The façade comprises a curtain wall of steel, glass and polished red granite. The striking feature of this type of construction is the fact that the natural stone was cut extremely thin and set into the steel structure as panels. This permitted a considerable degree of prefabrication.

Thus, it was possible to hang complete façade elements, including the glass panes, on steel anchors sunk in the concrete base and supports. On the pyramid at the top of the building, however, the glass panes were glued together to create an impermeable surface.

Entry façade

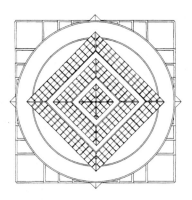

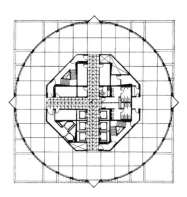

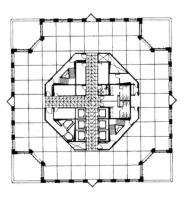

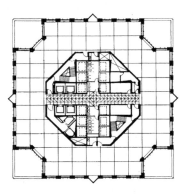

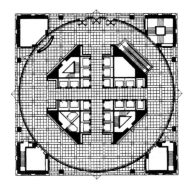

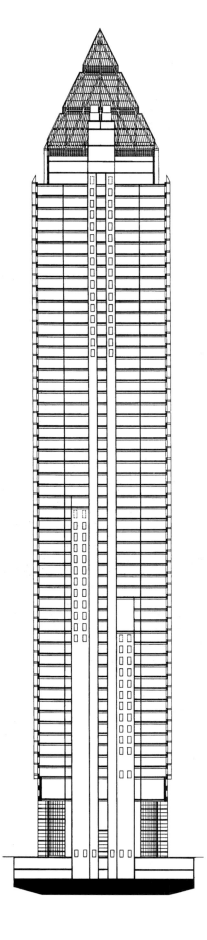

NEC SUPER TOWER

Location	Tokyo, Japan
Architect	Nikken Sekkei Planners, Architects and Engineers
Completion	1990
Height	186 m (610 ft)
Volume	ca 500 000 m³
Use	Office

Urban context
The Nec Super Tower stands in a densely built-up district of Tokyo in the midst of what are, for the most part, low buildings. The lower section of the Nec Super Tower is level with the neighbouring buildings and thus closely integrated into its surroundings. The upper section soars above the surrounding buildings, constituting a reference point in the area.

Structure
The stacking of variously formed ground plans on top of one another required the development of an autonomous bearing structure. The core zones at both ends of the tower contain lifts, wet areas and stairs, and create the effect of continuous box-shaped columns. The trussed girders running between the two core zones form a massive 3-storey "super frame". This bearing structure does away with the need for a secondary structure that would otherwise have been required to form the atrium and the large opening in the middle section of the building. The existing structure allows for the integration of spatial units of different heights.

162

Circulation / Installations

In order to allow for maximum compatibility with future technical advances, horizontal and vertical duct zones have been included and form a three-dimensional grid servicing the entire building. This makes it possible to respond quickly to new requirements at every point of the building.

Façade

The large opening between the lower and middle sections of the building is 42 m wide and 15 m high and serves as a large draught lobby. Here, the air currents moving down the façade are collected and redirected. This prevents winds from moving further down and adversely affecting neighbouring buildings and pedestrians on the streets. The opening also serves as a large window allowing light into the interior via the 14-storey atrium. Like the Landmark Tower in Yokohama, the Tower is noted for its narrow strip windows, which give the building a compact, untouchable appearance. As in Yokohama, this effect is balanced by enormous interior worlds within the building.

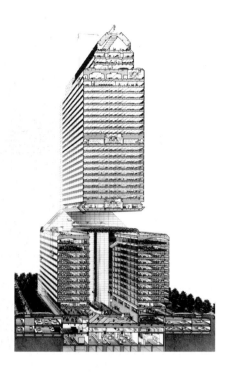
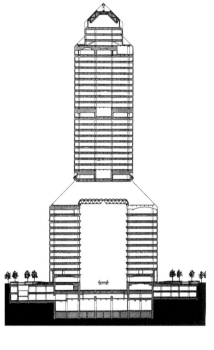

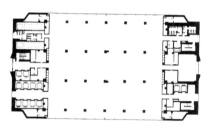

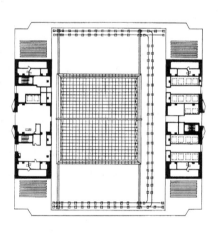
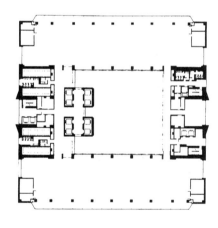

CANARY WHARF TOWER

Location	London, Great Britain
Architect	Cesar Pelli & Associates
Structural Engineer	M.S. Yolles & Partners
Completion	1991
Height	244 m (800 ft)
Volume	ca 700 000 m³
Use	Services, offices

Urban context

The Canary Wharf Tower (now called One Canada Square) was England's first skyscraper. It rises 50 storeys over the Docklands area, around 5 km away from central London. The idea behind the Canary Wharf Tower stems from the simple and traditional urban plan used in the city.

Public spaces have a symmetrical design, with their axes leading to the main entrance of the building. On the ground floor, there are restaurants and bars; the upper stories are used as office space. The Canary Wharf Tower has the sheer form of a monumental obelisk with a pyramid-shaped crown. Cesar Pelli decided to use a "quadratic ground plan with a pyramid crown, since this is a familiar shape in every culture." Despite the Canary Wharf Tower being what might be called a mega-venture, it does not in fact have a mega-structure.

Structure

The foundations of the tower, 4.5 m thick, rest on 222 pillars, each 1.8 m in diameter, and sunk to a depth of 20 m below the ground floor. A fine steel construction stands on the foundations. Great care was taken to ensure that the steel construction had the optimal structure needed for the building to easily absorb the effects of any sudden strong gusts of wind.

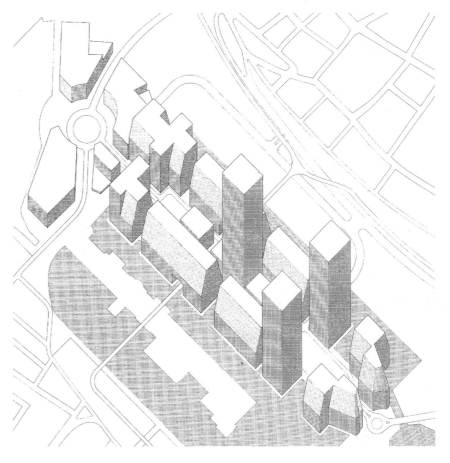

Circulation / Installations

The installations are located in the centre of the building, thus allowing the floor areas to be provided with the maximum amount of natural light. All the floor areas have been designed and connected in the same way.

Façade

The façade is uniform over the whole building, and the frequent changes in the London sky are constantly reflected in the stainless steel cladding and windows. The height and monolithic position of Canary Wharf Tower as part of the London skyline both lend it a monumental appearance and have provided a model for later developments.

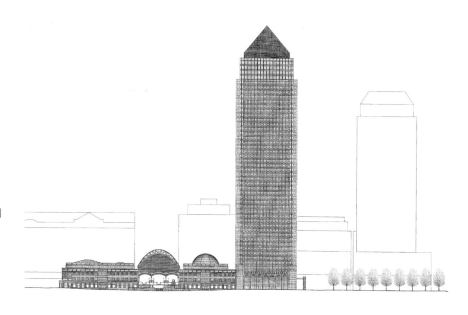

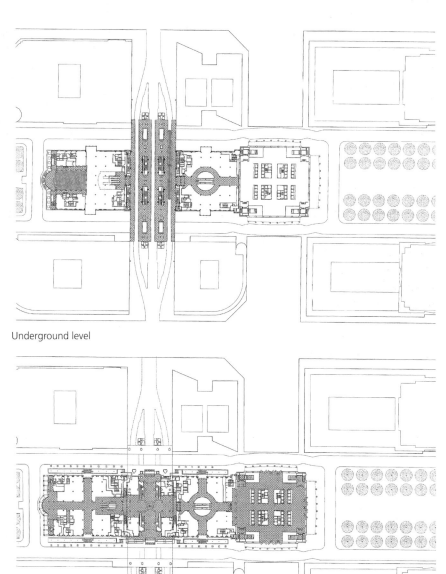

Underground level

Street level

CENTURY TOWER

Location	Tokyo, Japan
Architect	Norman Foster & Partners
Structural Engineer	Ove Arup & Partners
Completion	1991
Height	136 m (446 ft)
Volume	ca 100 000 m³
Use	Offices, museum, sports club, restaurant, apartments

Urban context

The Century Tower is located near a main arterial road and a railway line running through Tokyo's Bunkyo-Ku district, a historical area with primarily low-level buildings. The entire plot was used for the building, whose underground plinth contains a museum, restaurant, sports club and swimming pool. Great importance was attached to giving the Century Tower a unique appearance. Transparency and stratification are used to evoke the spirit of Japan

Structure

The two towers are formed by two-storey blocks and are connected throughout by an impressive 71.3-m-high central atrium. The mezzanine floor is suspended from the principal load-bearing framework. In their use of the atrium, Foster & Partners have been able to create a completely open office building without the restrictions imposed by fixed interior installations or supports.

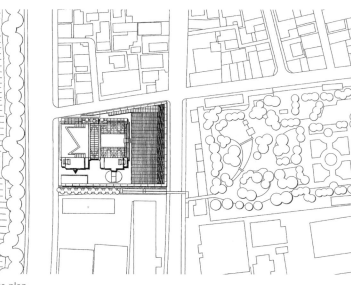

Site plan

Circulation / Installations

Servicing and served areas are distinctly separated. Fire escapes, service lifts and shafts, toilets and air-conditioning are all located in the east section. The elevators for office employees and visitors are located in the west façade. The centrally open atrium requires special fire prevention measures, and in the atrium itself there is constant excess pressure so the smoke can be extracted in case of fire.

Façade

The Century Tower's façade is dominated by the load-bearing framework. The form is the result of intensive research to develop a structure able to withstand both earthquakes and typhoons. The same requirement applied to the 2-storey-high windows, which, in addition to coping with normal wind loads, must be able to withstand much greater thrusts.

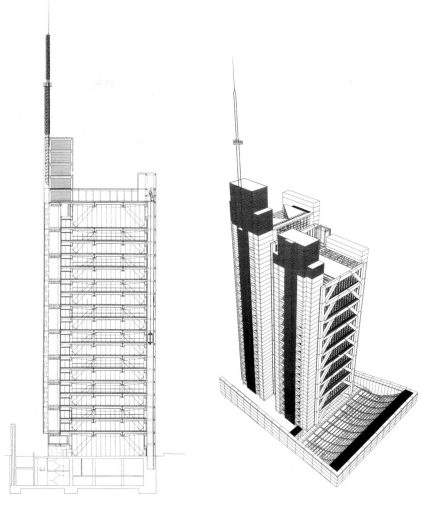

Section

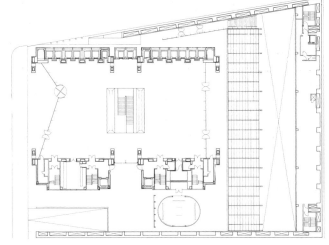

Ground floor

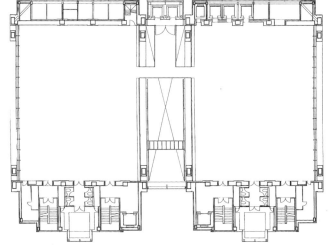

Typical storey

167

NEW TOKYO CITY HALL

Location	Tokyo, Japan
Architect	Kenzo Tange Associates
Structural Engineer	Mutoh Associates
Completion	1991
Height	243 m (797 ft)
Volume	ca 1 000 000 m³
Use	Office

Urban context

In 1986, the City of Tokyo held a competition on a design for a new city hall to replace the old building, dating from 1957, in the district of Marunouchi. Kenzo Tange's prize-winning project was an ensemble of two administrative buildings of forty-eight and thirty-six storeys plus a flat-roofed conference hall. The complex was to be constructed in the more easily accessible district of Shinjuku.

The blocks are grouped around a central plaza that holds 6 000 people. The tallest building has been divided into two quadratic towers at the thirty-second floor to avoid an overly massive appearance and establish a relationship with the other tall structures in the area.

The 7-storey aluminium-clad conference hall with colonnades encloses the semicircular public plaza. Bordered on all sides by abstract figures, the plaza slopes gently towards a central stage. Kenzo Tange, who sees himself as an urban architect, has constantly returned to designing urban structures during the course of his creative career. For Tokyo City Hall, he consciously accentuated the public function of the complex by attempting to include the vital aspect of interpersonal communication, which is often painfully absent in a vast city like Tokyo, where commuters spend hours travelling to and from work.

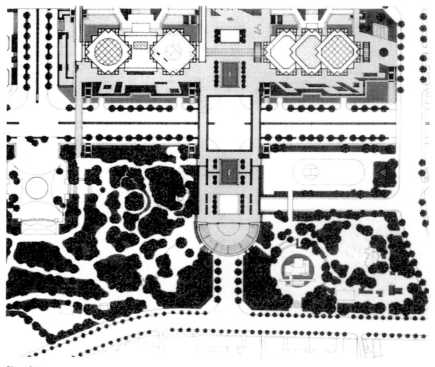

Site plan

Structure

The superstructure allows clear spanning of 19.2 m, thus creating column-free spaces for modern office areas and flexible areas for meetings, receptions, terminals, etc. Mobile wall systems make rearrangement of the office areas a simple matter, whilst the presence of corner windows and spacious green areas creates a feeling of comfort and well-being among users.

Circulation / Installations

The vertical access points of the twin towers are located at the corners of the cross-shaped plan. In the lower part of the building, they take up the entire rear side of the building.

Façade

In his façade design, Kenzo Tange employed the basic forms of traditional Japanese architecture: or mullion and transom section. The resemblance between his horizontal and vertical window lines and electronic circuits inspired him to accentuate both the microchip element and technoid character of the façade in order to create a contemporary work of architecture corresponding to the computerised society of today.

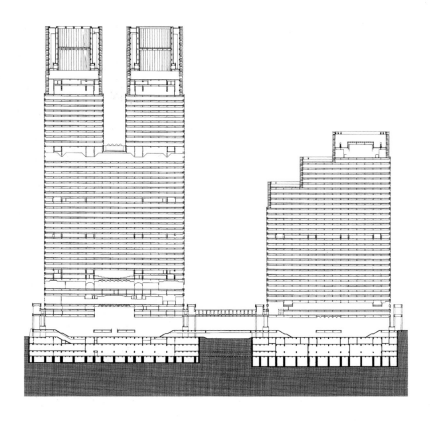

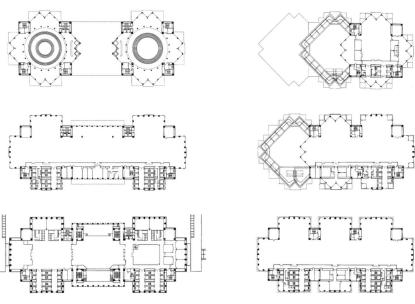

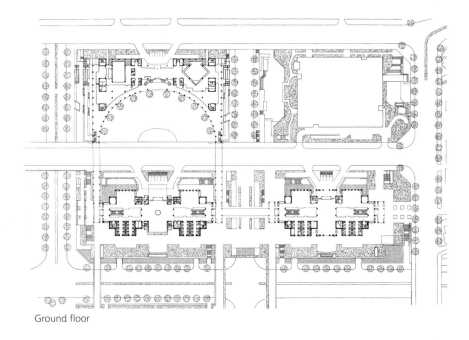

Ground floor

NATIONSBANK CORPORATE CENTER

Location	Charlotte, NC, USA
Architect	Cesar Pelli & Associates
Structural Engineer	W.P. Moore & Ass.
Completion	1992
Height	265 m (871 ft)
Volume	ca 700 000 m³
Use	Office

Urban context

The tower of the NCNB headquarters, the highest in the southeast USA, rises above the geographic, historic and economic centre of downtown Charlotte. Envisaged by the developers as a symbol of success and profit, the architect Ceasar Pelli was able to take this concept and create a successful example of including public claims in a private building scheme.

In order to maintain a unique presence in the cityscape and revive the inner city area, a range of public amenities were integrated into the planning, including a hotel, two theatres, landscaped plazas and "Founder's Hall", which consists of a large, glass-roofed public space lined with shops and boutiques.

The North Carolina performing Arts Center contains a 2100-seat theatre and a smaller 450-seat venue with the necessary infrastructural facilities. Access to the theatre area is through a semi-circular, zenithally illuminated foyer. Apart from the N. Tryon St. side of the complex, where the entrances and access road to the tower and the large theatre are located, the remainder of the complex can only be reached via three pedestrian bridges and from the underground parking area.

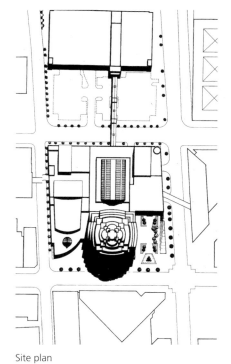

Site plan

Structure

The developers' initial concept was of a building which would be optimal in terms of height, economy and spatial efficiency. As a result, concrete poured in place was used to reduce floor-to-floor height and create an optimal span from core to perimeter. At the same time, this technique ensured lower costs than would have been the case with a combined steel skeleton and reinforced concrete structure.

Circulation / Installations

Access to the tower is via the access road on the corner of N. Tyron St. and E. Trade St. The spacious lobby includes twenty-two lifts and two emergency stairways. The areas connected with the tower are supplied via a complex and even bewildering circulation system on the ground floor.

Façade

The main façades are slightly curved and stepped back as the tower rises. The plinth is clad in black granite and the entrance framed by black marble columns. The pronounced use of stone on the lower floors stands for the stability of the building and – hopefully – of the company, too. The vertically oriented window apertures, surrounded by beige granite, underscore the builder's desire to draw the gaze of the observer upwards, over each of the set-backs to the almost gothic-style finial, where an ingeniously illuminated crown dominates the skyline of Charlotte by night.

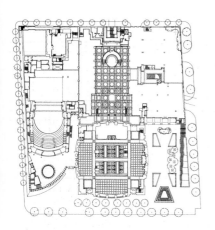

Ground floor

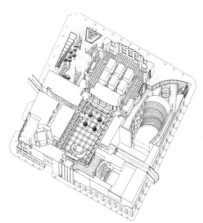

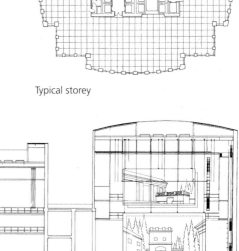

Typical storey

Longitudinal section plinth

DG BANK – HEADQUARTERS

Location	Frankfurt, Germany
Architect	Kohn, Pedersen, Fox & Associates
Completion	1993
Height	201 m (660 ft)
Volume	ca 280 000 m³
Use	Services, office and residential

Urban context

The DG Bank is located between the residential area of Frankfurt Westend and a commercial district. Each side of the building enters into a dialogue with its surroundings. The north side of the granite-clad plinth faces the residential district, whilst the west and south sides look towards the commercial district.

The DG Bank building combines diverse elements. The office tower, which establishes the upper limit of the surrounding tower blocks, is composed of a stone cube facing the residential district and a glass semicircle opposite the commercial district. The crown faces the Old City and Frankfurt Cathedral. An L-shaped plinth hugs the tower, creating a graduated transition between the office tower and the residential district. Between the two structures, there is a covered winter garden, which serves as an arcade and city loggia. The building, whose ground floor is open to the public, extends the city area.

Structure

The office tower is a tube-in-tube structure. The inner tubes of the solid load-bearing twin tube serve as the installation core, the outer as a punctuated façade. The floor slabs are fixed to the tubes. The L-shaped plinth is supported by a conventional pier-and-girder system to which the floor slabs are fixed.

Circulation / Installations

The technical installations are located on the fifth and thirty-ninth floors. Four lift towers of varying height mark the corners of the complex. Each of the lifts is flanked by supply shafts.

Façade

The curtain-wall façade is clad in glass and aluminium. Its minimalist design reflects an attempt to accentuate both the volume and the building materials. Graphic horizontal bands run across the glass surface, whilst the windows of the punctuated façade are provided with slightly projecting glazing bars, thus ensuring that the maximum amount of light enters the rooms and creating a sense of depth.

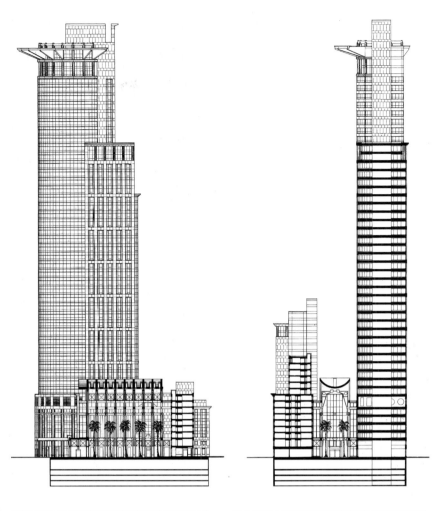

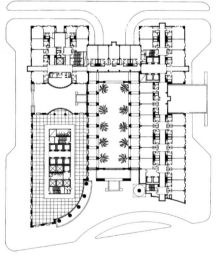

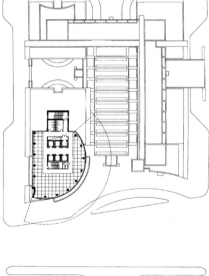

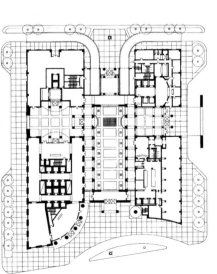

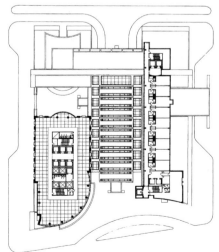

LANDMARK TOWER

Location	Yokohama, Japan
Architect	The Stubbins Associates and Mitsubishi Estate Co., Ltd.
Structural Engineer	Le Messurier Consultants Inc.
Completed	1993
Height	296 m (972 ft)
Volume	ca 1 400 000 m³
Use:	Commercial, office, hotel, restaurant

Urban context

The Landmark Tower is the highest building in Japan and was consciously built as an architectural urban highlight, the actual and symbolic gateway to the country. At the same time, the Landmark Tower is by far the highest building in Yokohama and, with its futuristic design, an outstanding feature in the region. At street level, the building is connected to the city via a large shopping centre, stretching from the second storey at basement level to the fifth storey above ground, and contains a 200-meter-long, 5-story atrium. The plan shows the 70-storey tower as a rectangle with projecting exterior corners whose depth decreases towards the top of the building. The Landmark Tower is a mixed-use complex with an observation floor (the Skygarden) and a restaurant at the very top, underneath which there is a 15-storey hotel with 600 beds. The building, whose design does justice to its function as a landmark, is open to the public.

Structure

The Landmark Tower is a steel construction, built as a steel truss tube with mega-columns. A central core constitutes the interior of the tower while the exterior is formed by four specially shaped tubular corner sections filled with concrete. The building contains a special "vibration-reducing mechanism" to equalise vibrations caused by extremely strong wind forces, which can be considerably greater than those of earthquakes.

Circulation / Installations

Vertical access is provided by thirty-nine elevators, which, together with the other elements of the infrastructure, are located in the core. Access to the office areas and the hotel (which is served by seven lifts) is separate.

Façade

The façade, constructed after the curtain wall principle, consists of natural stone slabs and glass. The 1:1 height ratio between the horizontal glass bands and strips of granite makes the latter stand out and lends the tower a sturdy appearance. The architects have successfully achieved a synthesis between the high culture of sophisticated traditional Japanese craftsmanship and contemporary art: the simple grace of the hair comb, the precision in dovetailing wood, and the translucency of the paper lantern have all contributed to the successful composition of this granite-clad skyscraper.

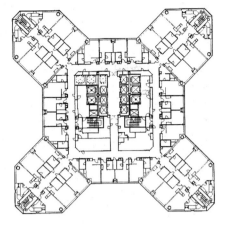
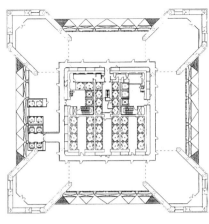

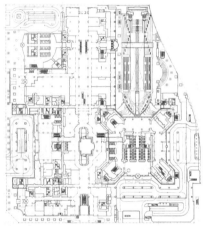

Ground floor

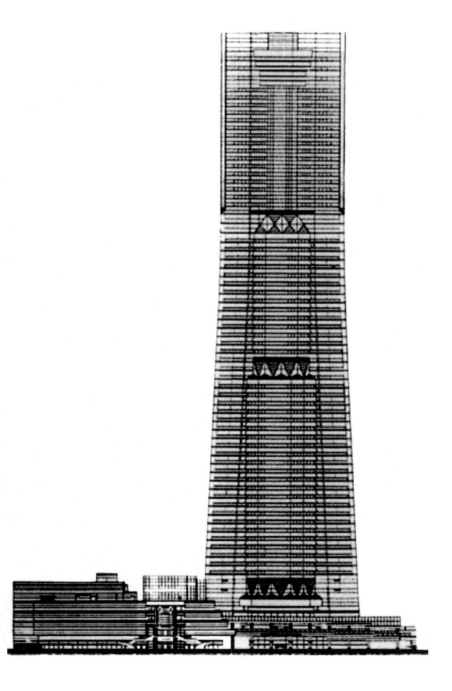

UMEDA SKY BUILDING

Location	Osaka, Japan
Architect	Hiroshi Hara and Atelier
Structural Engineer	Toshihiko Kimura
Completion	1993
Height	173 m (568 ft)
Volume	ca 600 000 m³
Use	Office, multiple

Urban context

The Umeda Sky Building can be considered a Japanese-style attempt to take up the theme of la Grande Arche in La Défense, Paris. This 40-storey bridge-like building functions as a kind of entrance to, and symbol for, the new Umeda District in Osaka. However, such a comparison is probably somewhat superficial, since the two buildings not only differ in size, but are also located in totally contrasting urban situations. Hiroshi Hara's building is, above all else, a prototype in a city of verticals, in which all skyscrapers are linked by escalators, lifts, passages, terraces and roof gardens within a network of three-dimensional public spaces. With his solution, which is reminiscent of a "space odyssey", the architect has thematised the problem of adding yet another urban structure to a location already crowded with buildings.

Without the painstaking development of the materials, the interior spaces, the connections between interior and exterior, and the passages, the building would have remained nothing more than a spectacle. That it turned out otherwise is also the merit of an architectural competition, the selection of this rather unusual project, and the coherent realisation of the architectural design. In addition, the developer commissioned the creation of public areas such as an esplanade, gardens, fountains and ornamental lakes, sculptures and, within the building itself, an art centre, restaurants and a shopping gallery.

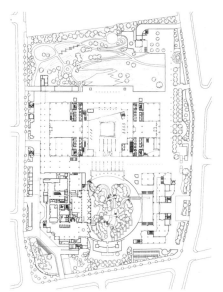

Ground floor

176

Structure

The building has a conventional load-bearing structure, with the vertical load-transfer in the external areas and reinforcing core areas on the interior. The bridges are steel frame structures.

Circulation / Installations

Vertical access, such as stairs and lifts, has been arranged inside the two towers, making it possible to construct the office sections as clear-span, open areas within the glazed outer walls. A freestanding lift tower allows passengers to experience the full height of the interspace.

Façade

The various, almost allegorical, elements that comprise "Mid-Air-City" (the space between the "individual" skyscrapers) are reflected endlessly in the glazed curtain-wall façade. In the reflection of the various materials – glass, aluminium and concrete – the tower walls create illusions of a densely constructed imaginary city that blends with the reflections of the real city all around. At night, the "floating crater" conjures up the image of a space-ship about to land above the immense void below.

The building signals the dawn of a new era of skyscraper architecture, a style born of progress that unites building technologies and the conceptual construction of multifunctional high-rise buildings.

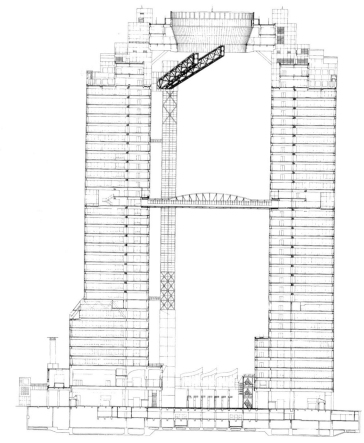

Longitudinal section

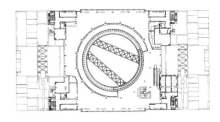

40th floor

22nd floor

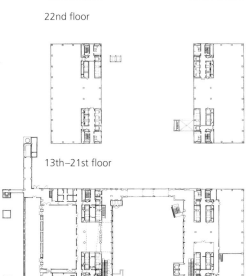

13th–21st floor

3rd floor

TOUR CRÉDIT LYONNAIS

Location	Lille, France
Architect	Christian de Portzamparc
Completion	1995
Height	130 m (426 ft)
Volume	87 000 m³
Use	Office

Urban context

The Crédit Lyonnais building is part of the extensive Euralille urban project aiming to establish the city in northern France as a European trade and communications centre in the Paris-Brussels-London triangle. It stands in a row of three towers designed as bridge buildings spanning the newly erected TGV station. The row is to be extended to the south-east to include five more slender towers on plinths. Their arrangement corresponds with a second row of shorter towers whose ground plans tend to be more quadratic. The voluminous newly built shopping centre, designed by Rem Koolhaas (who also designed the master plan for the project), stretches between the two axes. The sculptural structure is a variation on the theme of the "tower on a plinth". In the illustration, the latter is also presented as a bridge.

Structure

The vertical loads are transferred by partially inclined reinforced concrete pillars flush with the façade and positioned in the centre of the plan, as well as by the two cores, which provide reinforcement, too. Binding beams and floor sheets take care of the horizontal transfer and reinforcement. The cores are partly inserted into the tower plinth and the "supporting buildings", where they assume the form of "bridge piers" supporting a box girder (h=3.2 m). The box girder absorbs the load of cross-girders cantilevered on both sides, on which the columns of the plinth and the tower rest.

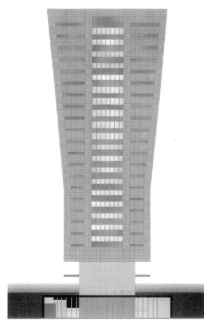

Circulation / Installations

The sanitation system, installation shafts and circulation are concentrated in the two inner cores. There are four lifts for the tower and two for the plinth.

Façade

The various parts of the building are distinguished from one another by façades of varying materials, colours and proportions. The plinth and the tower have been given a uniform sculptural appearance, whilst the inclined façade is clad in grey-green metal panels and windows accentuating the overall form of the building. On the inner side of the L-shape, the building has a curtain-wall in the form of a mullion-and-transom façade, which can be interpreted as a sectional area of the fragmented structure. It has apparently been designed in this way to allow users an optimal view of the old city centre. The green-tinted floor-to-ceiling glazing harmonises with the metal cladding of the punctuated façade. In both cases, interior solar protection is provided by venetian blinds. Contrast is provided by the natural stone cladding of the supporting buildings.

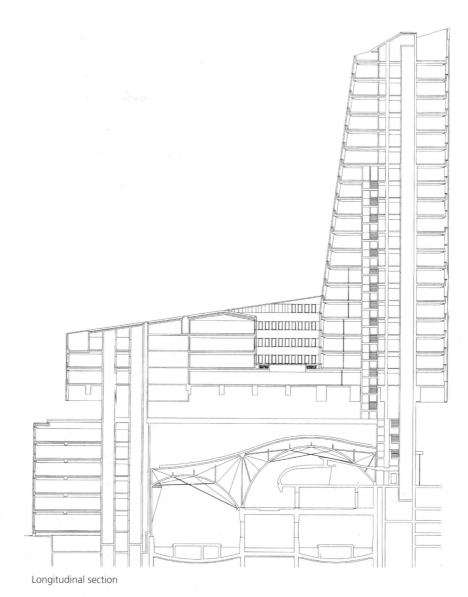

Longitudinal section

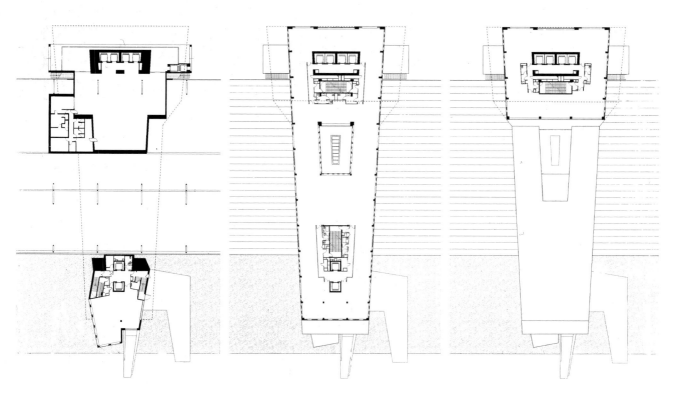

COMMERZBANK

Location	Frankfurt, Germany
Architect	Norman Foster & Partners
Structural Engineer	Ove Arup & Partners
Completion	1997
Height	259 m (850 ft)
Volume	ca 450 000 m³
Use	Bank, offices, restaurant, shops

Urban context

The city was in favour of having the building set back from the street, but the architect wanted to show that the tower was rooted to the ground. Finally, as a compromise, the conventional block edge facing Kaiserplatz was left completely sealed. Only a small passage leads to the raised gallery at the foot of the tower whose 29-m shaft can be seen in its full majesty from Zur Grossen Gallusstrasse. The confined urban space on this side of the street has created a density hitherto unknown to Frankfurt, but no longer so far removed from the Manhattan model of a street lined by skyscrapers.

Structure

The reinforced principal bearing structure is situated behind the façade. Together with the 8-storey Vierendeel beams, the two reinforced composite columns at each of the rounded corners create a rigid frame. Firmly held in a 3-storey reinforced concrete box in the ground-floor and basement area, it forms a rigid tube. This structure and the girders at the sides of the atrium support the continuous steel beams on which the floors rest. These beams, in turn, are fixed to the concrete floors by means of headed studs and profiled sheet to form a reinforced connecting slab at every fourth storey. Being light in comparison with reinforced concrete, the steel structure allows clear-span offices with flexible floor areas.

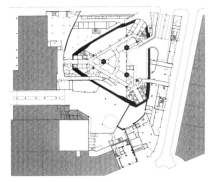

Ground floor

Circulation / Installations

The building has a double façade with adjustable solar shading. The gardens and the atrium create well-aired room zones around the office areas, thus keeping out disturbing environmental influences such as traffic noise, dazzle and overheating due to direct sunlight, as well as excluding the wintry cold, winds and the weather. They thus create a healthy climate within the building and permit natural, individually adjustable ventilation and illumination of all the interior rooms. Energy loss is kept to a minimum. The utility operating costs are relatively low, since the heating, mechanical ventilation and waste-air extraction as well as the chilled-water ceiling panels need only be switched on to supplement natural sources when weather conditions are adverse. Vertical shafts containing the lifts and emergency staircases provide access to the rest of the building; these shafts, which also contain the installations, are located in the rounded corners of the triangular plan.

Façade

The building owes its striking appearance to the solid, rounded corners as well as the multi-storey stacks of offices suspended between them and separated vertically by glazed garden terraces, which were originally intended to be open. The façade's technoid appearance is created by a surface composed entirely of glass, steel and aluminium.

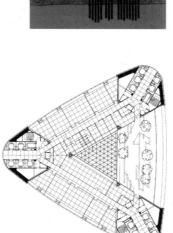
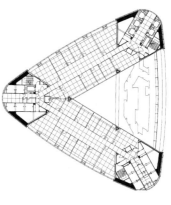

Typical office storeys

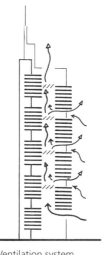

Ventilation system

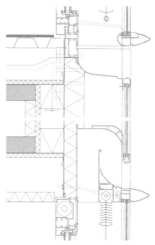

Façade detail

PETRONAS TOWERS

Location	Kuala Lumpur, Malaysia
Architect	Cesar Pelli & Associates
Structural Engineer	Thornton-Tomasetti, Ranhill Bersekutu
Completion	1997
Height	452 m (1482 ft)
Volume	ca 3 000 000 m³
Use	Office, shops, entertainment

Urban context

The 88-storey Petronas Towers are located in a green area in Kuala Lumpur. The centre, owned by the state-owned Petronas mineral-oil company, is used by businesses, offices and residents, as well as for leisure activities. As many as 50 000 people travel to there every day. An underground line provides rapid transport to other parts of the city.

The unique height of the two slender towers (which have a diameter of thirty m) and the horizontal axis of the pedestrian bridge linking the forty-second storeys (which induced the architect to speak of a "portal to the sky") have made the Petronas Towers into an urban gateway. These features, together with the brightly shining silhouette of the towers, have given Kuala Lumpur a new symbol. The design of the ground plan, which was created through complex repetitions of the basic figure, shows great respect for traditional Islamic culture. This is also reflected in the use of geometric forms in the design as a whole.

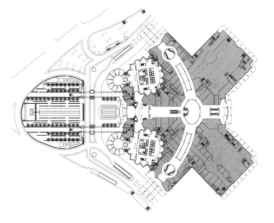

Ground floor

Structure

The vertical loads are transferred by a central concrete core and round concrete columns. The supports are inclined to allow for the set-backs at floors sixty, seventy-three and eighty-two, thus rendering load-transferring beams superfluous. Horizontal forces are absorbed by the round concrete girders linking the core and the columns. The structure of the 58-m-long, two-level bridge consists of parallel steel girders.

Circulation / Installations

The installations are housed in the core of the Petronas Towers to facilitate the allocation of space.

Each tower has a lift lobby on the ground floor. Conventional lifts take the passengers to the lower storeys, whilst an express lift ascending to the sky lobby serves the upper storeys. On arrival in the sky lobby, passengers can change to a conventional lift.

Façade

The façade was especially designed to shield the rooms from the intense rays of the tropical sun. Room shadow has been created by both setting back the storeys and making certain modifications to the façade, which is composed of glass bands and stainless steel panels. The use of stainless steel magnifies the reflection of the intense rays of the tropical sun and gives the building a timeless appearance.

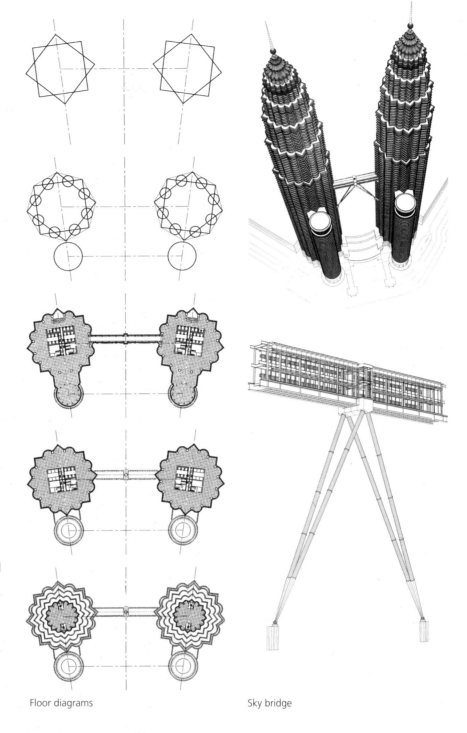

Floor diagrams

Sky bridge

PLAZA 66 BUILDING

Location	Shanghai, China
Architect	Kohn Pedersen Fox & Associates
Structural Engineer	Thornton-Tomasetti Engineers
Completion	2000
Height	281 m (923 ft)
Volume	ca 1 200 000 m^3
Use	Multiple, office

Urban context

The Plaza 66 complex, currently under construction and known locally as Nanjing Xi Lu, stands on the busiest shopping street in Shanghai inner city. It is designed for a mixture of shops and offices. As with many skyscrapers constructed in the Far East in recent years, its significance for the urban surroundings is to be sought less in contextual references or in its architectural statement than in the building's function as a catalyst to the future development of Shanghai as one of the most important financial and cultural centres in Asia during the twenty-first century.

One of the plinth zones contains the shops. The offices are located in the two towers, the tallest of which is sixty-six storeys high and the lowest forty-seven.

The shopping area is arranged along a five-storey-high podium, which imitates the scale of historical Chinese streets. Open rooms, flooded by light, are situated at each end: a five-story lens-shaped atrium lined with galleries, and a fully glazed rotunda – both inviting visitors to stay a while. A conspicuous feature of Plaza 66 is the unusual formal language – for skyscrapers at least – of the individual structures, as their use of forms reveals an attempt to draw on ultramodern styles involving diagonals, curves, undulations, etc., and to relate them to the functional demands of a high-rise building.

Site plan

Structure

The load-bearing structure corresponds to present-day standards. Up to the façade, the building has clear-span floors arranged around a reinforcing core.

Circulation / Installations

Vertical access inside the tower is provided by eighteen passenger and two goods lifts situated at the centre. This zone also contains the shafts and secondary rooms.

Façade

Although the street entrances separate the main functions, the overall volumetric design has created a unified, massed composition. Two towers clad in aluminium and glass flank the curved plinth. The use of stone cladding on the lower storeys lends the building the solidity necessary to establish a visual counterweight to the high towers. At the apex, almost 300 m above the ground, the complex is punctuated by a lantern of billowing screens that is designed to glow over the city at night.

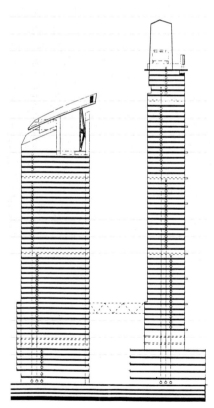

Longitudinal section

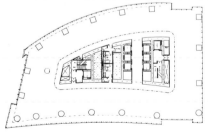
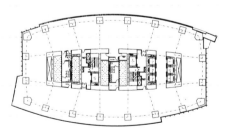

Typical storey

MENARA TELEKOM TOWER

Location	Kuala Lumpur, Malaysia
Architect	Hijjas Kasturi Associates
Structural Engineer	Ranhill Bersekutu
Completion	2000
Height	310 m (1017 ft)
Volume	ca 600 000 m³
Use	Multiple, office

Urban context

Situated along the Federal Highway, the new head office of the Menara Telekom Group stands at the entrance to the city centre of Kuala Lumpur. Furthermore, the project is adjacent to the newly opened light rail transit system, which is now in operation and allows for rapid commuting from the complex to downtown.

The Menara Telekom building is among the country's most stunning pieces of recent architecture, displaying an elliptical tower 310 m high. Its realisation involved combining an economic and functional workplace with technological requirements and the high-tech nature of the telecommunications industry. It also had to create a remarkable and civic-style symbol of the technical growth of the country itself. The Malaysian sculptor and painter Latiff Mohidin influenced deeply the shape of the building with his sketch of "pucuk rebung": "a new sprout of bamboo shooting from the earth, anchored by solid roots, and the beauty of an unfurling leaf". This "organic" nature had to be harmonised with the technical necessities of easy construction and planning efficiency. It was also important that the site be treated as a park open to the public, with landscaped terraces, open plazas, seating areas and water ornamentation.

Flanking the tower on the east is a well-equipped auditorium for concert performances. Located below the audi-

torium is a theme park with an exhibition hall, a small theatre, a fully computerised library, a TV studio and various workspaces.

A spacious multi-purpose hall is situated on the opposite edge of the site and surrounded by a landscaped courtyard for sports and recreation activities, as well as a medical and a childcare centre. The tower itself will incorporate the most advanced state-of-the-art intelligent building systems. It can also hold a working population of about 6 000 and has space for expansion in 21st century.

Structure

The loads are transferred along the lense-shaped ground figure via columns in the façade. Two tower shells of different height arise from the central reinforced core to a height of 77 storeys that are linked to one another by the framework of the Sky Gardens. The smaller of the two shells is linked at the top to a round platform that serves as a helicopter landing-pad.

Circulation / Installations

Thirty-five Schindler elevators transport the 5 700 employees. To efficiently move so many people, eighteen double-deck elevators in three groups (six per group) are assigned to three different zones – low, mid and high – in the 50-storey building: The double deck elevators carry a load of 2 x 1 360 kg and reach speeds from 3.5 to 6 m/s. To use the full transport capacity of these elevators, there are two boarding levels, connected with escalators, on the main floors. Each double-deck elevator serves the main floors, with the upper deck stopping at the ground floor and the lower deck stopping at the lower ground floor.

Façade

Sky gardens with amenities for relaxation are provided at every third floor. Complementing the tower's high-tech external façade, each of the twenty-two sky gardens serves as a living filter regulating heat, light and noise for the comfort of the employees working inside.

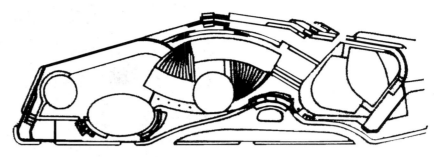

Site plan

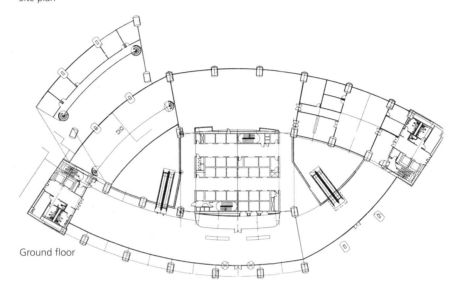

Ground floor

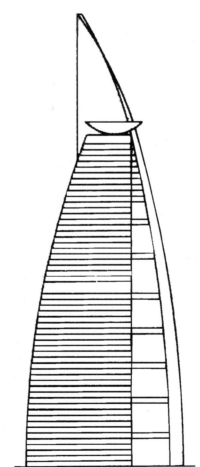

Structure diagram

88 PHILIP STREET OFFICE TOWER & MACQUARIE APARTMENTS

Location	Sydney, Australia
Architect	Renzo Piano Building Workshop
Structural Engineer	Lend Lease Design Group, Ove Arup & Partners
Completion	2000
Height	200 m (656 ft)
Volume	ca 400 000 m³
Use	Commercial and residential

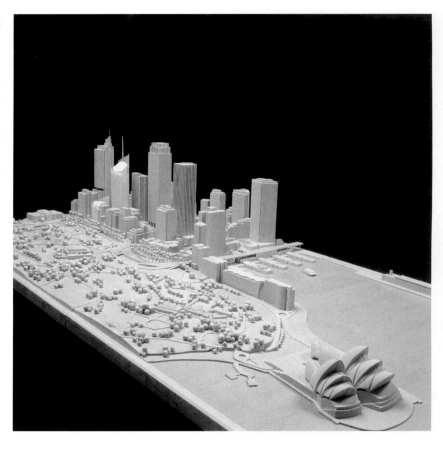

Urban context

In connection with the Olympic Games in 2000 in Sydney, the Lend Lease Development Company awarded a contract for a high-rise complex. It consists of two structures, a 44-storey office tower and a 17-storey residential building linked at street level by a glass-covered square to form an urban microcosm. The composition is located in the historical district of the city alongside other high-rise buildings, and stands next to the city park leading down to the Sydney Opera House designed by Jørn Utzon.

In order to do justice to this world-famous urban symbol, particular attention was given to the architectural detail of the new building. As a consequence, in approaching the formal aspects of the building, the architects focused on the theme of the wind and the sea. Overlapping, vaulted, façade elements are positioned along lens-shaped plans. On the vertical plane, these elements form giant sails, which together assume the form of an open fan.

The architects also faced another challenge: that of creating a user-friendly environment in which residents and office-workers could live and work undisturbed. Winter gardens and terraces, functioning as recreational spaces, bring together users from all the different sections of the building, creating optimal recuperative areas that provide both shelter and a unique view of Sydney Harbour.

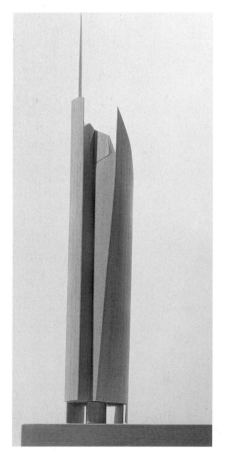

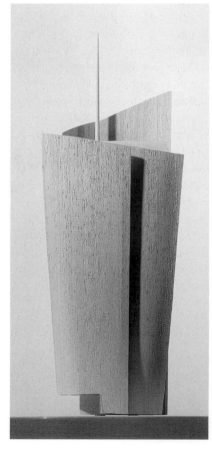

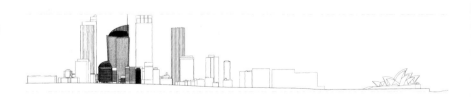

Structure

A massive, centrally positioned core of reinforced concrete distributes the load within the structure and provides horizontal stiffening. Mighty reinforced concrete columns of up to 1.4 m x 1.4 m transfer the loads of the floor slabs and the façades. The span between the columns is approximately 10 m.

Circulation / Installations

The lens-shaped core in the office tower has nineteen lift units, which carry passengers to low, middle or high-rise sections of the building. In the middle of the building there are two sets of fire-escape stairs which do not lead to street level, but are connected via a terrace with two additional laterally positioned external stairways. The core also houses the sanitation and the equipment zones, thus creating open space between the core and the façade.

Façade

The outer shell of the eastern and western façades consists of storey-high structural glazing elements: glass sheeting partly covered with an imprinted network of white points. According to the architects from RPBW, it was important "to give the design a delicate, free shape, as captured in the shell-like slope of the main façades. The fritted glass 'skin' of the building regulates the sun's rays and wall temperatures, while taking on a homogeneous cream-white, ghostly pallor. This glass skin extends beyond the building volume, dissolving its edges, and accentuating the building's overall lightness."

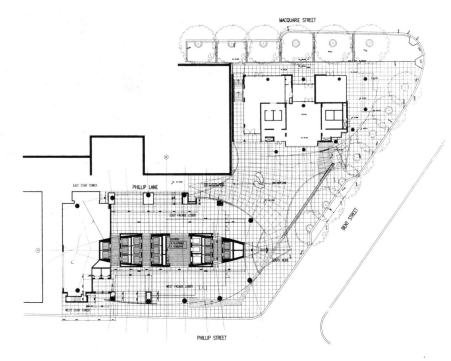

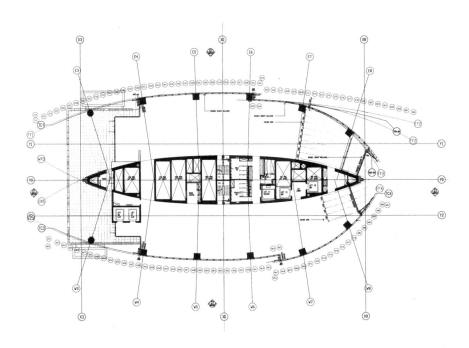

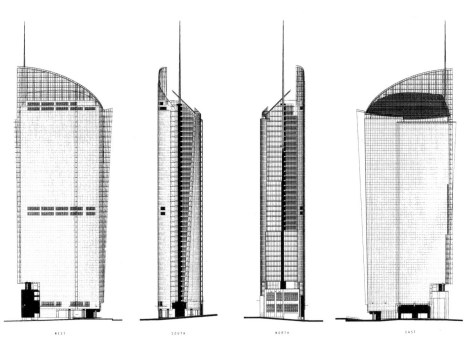

SWISS RE TOWER

Location	London, Great Britain
Architect	Norman Foster and Partners
Structural Engineer	Ove Arup & Partners
Completion	2003
Height	179.8 m (590 ft)
Volume	ca 200 000 m³
Use	Office

Urban context

The 1.4-acre property lies in the heart of London's insurance district. The site benefits from a great choice of public transport links, many of the train connections being only a short distance on foot. Apart from the fact that only the badly damaged remains for the Baltic Exchange once stood on the site, a number of other considerations led to the decision to build a skyscraper just here. The location is exempt from height restrictions imposed by the city administration in view of the strategic views corridors of St. Paul's Heights and the Monument view corridors. Furthermore, it is situated within the perimeter for high buildings around Tower 42, the International Finance Centre, and does not have to observe any of the regulations of a conservation area.

Finally, there are no restrictions due to underground railway lines. The building itself is a freestanding tower standing in an open space bordered by a surrounding group of buildings. The location is upgraded by public squares and meeting places.

Structure

The star-shaped core is a standard reinforced concrete structure transferring the inner loads and providing horizontal stiffening. An interesting feature is the diagonally braced structure along the curved façade skin, which transfers the external forces and absorbs wind loads.

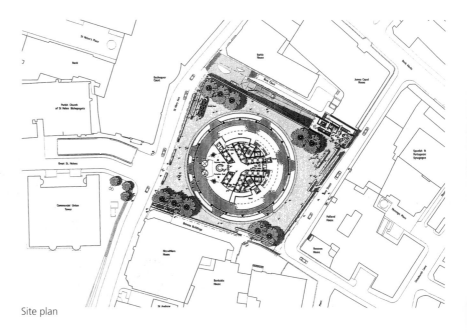

Site plan

Circulation / Installations

A corridor situated within the core provides access to the office areas on three sides. A total of sixteen lift units, as well as various service lifts and two fire-escape staircases, link the forty storeys to one another.

By rotating each successive floor, voids at the edge of each floor plate form a series of spiral atria. The aerodynamic form thus created has the advantage of generating natural ventilation, thanks to the immense difference in pressure arising within the building. The slats in the exterior cladding provide the rooms with additional air-conditioning. For the greater part of the year, the artificial cooling and ventilation systems can be switched off. On each floor, the atriums create a very comfortable micro-environment as well as vertical spatial continuity.

Façade

The external glazed skin of the building not only allows daylight to enter the building, but also provides for natural ventilation and acts as an acoustic buffer. Diagonal bands, triangular in shape, lend the Swiss Re Tower a unique appearance. According to Norman Foster, it is "a proposal which is radical – socially, technically, architecturally and spatially."

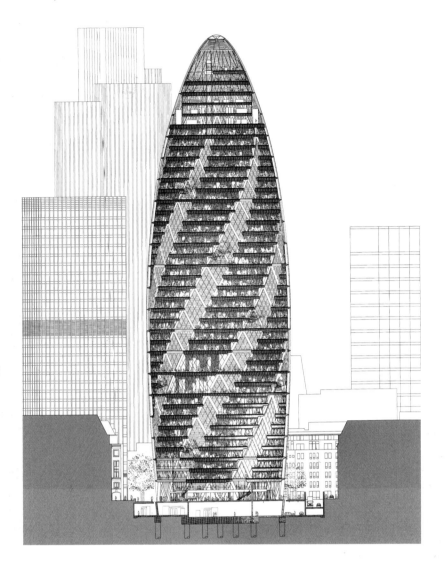

ACADEMIC YEAR COURSE 1997/1998

Professor   Prof. Mario Campi

Assistants Sibylle Bucher   Amr Soliman
                Dr. Paolo Fusi   Patrik Zurkirchen
                Uta Junghardt   Stefan Clavadetscher

Students   Stefanie Ammann   Marco Malacarne
                Philipp Anderegg   Nicole Manser
                Karin Baumann   Lukas Matter
                Urs Baumann   Corinna Menn
                Ivo Bertolo   Arne Mittig
                Thomas Birchmeier   Christian Naeff
                Reto Buchmann   Matthias Paetzold
                Philipp Büel   Vito Pantalena
                Oliver Burri   Carole Pax
                Alba Carint   Christian Peter
                Philippe Denier   Timon Reichle
                Konstanze Domhardt   Philipp Roesli
                Michael Eberle   Mark Rosa
                Justina Egli   Christian Rutishauser
                Anita Emele   Corinne Schaffner
                Christoph Fabbri   Marcel Scherrer
                Nadia Fistarol   Raphael Schmid
                Andreina Freimann   Thomas Schmid
                Antoine Frieders   Mathias Scholl
                Jutta Glanzmann   Stefania Schupp
                Stephen Griek   Sandra Schweizer
                Henrik Hansen   Sandra Sidler
                Hardy Happle   Antonella Sileno
                Stefan Hauser   Stauber Edward
                Katja Hauzinger   Nadja Tan
                Noriaki Hayakawa   Sarah Thury
                Christoph Helbich   Philipp Tscholl
                Lorenz Huber   Anelia Ulrich
                Roland Imboden   Christina Vegiopculou
                Lukas Imhof   Manuel Weber
                David Joho   Thomas Weiss
                Fawad Kazi   Esther Wicki
                Ivana Kordic   Martin Winkler
                Sebastian Leder   Simone Wyss
                Marc Liechti   Claudia Zehnder
                Nora Lippuner   Raphael Zuber
                Patrizia Maglie   Roman Zuest

ILLUSTRATION CREDITS

Ad'A: 86, 87: American Telephone and Telegraph courtesy of Rizzoli Publications, New York: 12 above; J. Apicella / Cesar Pelli & Associates: 182 above; Arcadia Edizioni: 104, 105 below, 114, 122, 123 below left; Courtesy of Architectures Jean Nouvel: 152, 153; Jamie Ardilles-Arce: 133 below right; Masao Arai: 32 above, 50 above, 88 above, 130, 140, 141, 170; Artemis: 66, 67 ; a+u: 18 below, 19 below, 23 middle right and below right, 26 above and below right, 32 below right; Morley Baer: 70; Steven Bergerson courtesy of Rizzoli Publications, New York: 150 above; Baumeister: 158, 159; Courtesy of Werner Blaser: 31 above and below left, 62 below left, 63 below left, 72 below left, 73 section and site, 91 above left; Boga: 118 below right, 119 below; Nicolas Borel courtesy of Christian de Portzamparc: 178; R. Bostwick / Cesar Pelli & Associates: 164 above; Cabanban courtesy of Rizzoli Publications, New York: 92 middle; Michael Carapetian: 54 above, below left; Casabella: 24 below, 27 schemes; il
Cardo Editore: 38 above, 39 above and below right; K. Champlin / Cesar Pelli & Associates: 137 model; Chicago Aerial Survey Co.: 30 above; Chicago Architectural Photographic Company: 90 below right; Peter Cook: 142 above; DAM courtesy of O.M. Ungers: 118 above; Richard Davies courtesy of Foster & Partners: 190 above; Courtesy of Editrice Abitare Segesta: 46, 47; Sigurd Fischer 20 middle left; FLW Foundation: 28, 29, 34, 35 middle and below, 36 below, 37 middle and below left; Foster and Partners: 134, 135 drawings, 148, 149, 180, 181 drawings; 190, 191; W. Fujii: 120, 121 below left; Y. Futagawa: 120 below, 131 middle left; Courtesy of Gangemi Editore: 115 below right; Brian Gassel 100 above; Dennis Gilbert courtesy of Rizzoli Publications, New York: 172 above; Janet Gill: 143 below right; John Gronkowski courtesy of Rizzoli Publications, New York: 57 middle right, 82 above; Oswald Grube: 139 below left; Harr for Hedrich-Blessing courtesy of Rizzoli Publications, New York: 75 below; Hedrich-Blessing courtesy of Murphy/Jahn: 62 above, 74 above; Hedrich-Blessing courtesy of Rizzoli Publications, New York: 30 below, 31 below right, 42 below, 57 middle left, 72 above, 74 below, 89 below right, 90 above and below left, 92 above and below; Courtesy of Hentrich / Petschnigg & Partners: 40, 41, 78, 79; Hijas Kasturi Associates Sdn courtesy of Schindler Lifts Company: 186, 187; Timothy Hursley, the Arkansas Office, courtesy of Rizzoli Publications, New York: 76 above, 102 above; 170; L. F. Inglada and H. Suzuki: 108 above, 109 below; JA: 174, 176, 177 below right; Howard N. Kaplan courtesy of Rizzoli Publications, New York: 43 above; KAPO / Shigeo Ogawa: 60 above, below left, 61 below right; Balthazar Korab courtesy of Rizzoli Publications, New York: 36 above, 89 above and below left, 150 below; Courtesy of Kohn Pedersen Fox: 125 above, 172 below, 173, 184, 185; Peter G. Kreitler, photograph collections: 10 below, 11; Ian Lambot: 134 above, 135 middle right, below left, 146, 147 below right, 166 above, 167 middle left,180, 181 below left; William Lescaze: 24 above; Eric Locker courtesy of Werk Bauen + Wohnen: 50 middle left; Loebl Schlossman

Hackl courtesy of Rizzoli Publications, New York: 102 below, 103; Norman McGrath from PAP / Manhattan Skyscraper: 10 above; Joseph W. Molitor: 80; Michael Moran: 52 above and below right, 156 above; Courtesy of Murphy/ Jahn: 62 middle and left, 63, 75 middle, 112, 113, 160, 161; MoMA New York: 91 middle and below left; Osamu Murai: 144 above, 145 below, 168 above and middle; New York Historical Society Collection: 14; Oxford University Press: 16, 17 below; Courtesy of Pei Cobb Freed: 94 below, 95, 98 below and 99, 138 below, 139, 154, 155, 157; Courtesy of Cesar Pelli: 129 above and below, 137, 151, 164 below, 165 right, 182, 183; Jeff Perkell courtesy of Rizzoli Publications, New York: 136; Courtesy of Renzo Piano Building Workshop: 188, 189; Courtesy of Phaidon: 37 above; John Portman & Associates: 101, 133; Michael W. Portman: 106, 107 above and below right, 132 above; Courtesy of Christian de Portzamparc: 178, 179; Cervin Robinson: 128, 129 middle; Courtesy of Kevin Roche John Dinkeloo and Associates: 64, 65, 96, 97; Rockefeller Center, Inc.: 26 below; Courtesy of Richard Rogers Partnership: 142, 143 drawings; Courtesy of Rizzoli Publications, New York: 126, 165 left; Steve Rosenthal: 98 below; Sy Rubin: 123 middle and below; E. Sierins courtesy of RPBW: 188 middle; Johann N. Schmidt: 98 above; SD: 144 below; Courtesy of Harry Seidler: 68, 69, 110, 111; Kouo-Shang Wei: 94 above, 95 below right; Courtesy of Skidmore, Owings & Merrill: 33, 42 below, 43, 49, 51, 71, 76 below, 77 above, 93, 116, 117; Malcolm Smith / Jane Doggett: 44 above; Henry Sowden and the flash of the facade by Ove Arup & Partners: 143 below left; Ezra Stoller ESTO courtesy of Rizzoli Publications, New York: 42 above, 44 below, 62 below right, 77 middle and below left, 93 middle right; Courtesy of The Stubbins Associates: 104, 105 above, 174, 175 above; Hisao Suzuki: 58 above, 59 above and middle right; Kenzo Tange & Associates: 145 below, 168 below, 169; Wayne Thom: 95 below left; Wes Thompson: 138 above; Thompson-Starrett: 20 above; Toomey: 54 below right; Urban Investments, a Division of JMB Realty courtesy of Rizzoli Publications, New York: 124 above, 125 below; Irving Underhill: 13 right below; Courtesy of O. M. Ungers: 118, 119 drawings; Wiss Janney Elstner Associates: 13 above left; S. Valastro courtesy of Werk Bauen + Wohnen: 32 below left; Courtesy of Werk Bauen + Wohnen 48 above and below right, 49, 50 below, 51, 57 below; Nick Wood / Hayes Davidson courtesy of Foster & Partners: 190 middle; 'World Cities, Tokyo' by Botond Bognar John Wiley & Sons Limited. Reproduced with permission: 84, 85, 148, 149 middle right, 162, 163, 167 middle right, 175 below right; Wurts Bros.-Photo: 18 above, 22; John Zukowsky courtesy of Rizzoli Publications, New York: 83 below left.

Grateful acknowledgement is given to those listed above permitting the use of their photographs and drawings. The author has made every possible effort to trace the original source of copyright material used in this publication. Any errors or omissions will be corrected in subsequent editions.